Joe Hill

The right of Simon Webb to be identified
as the Author of the Work has been asserted by
him in accordance with the Copyright, Designs
and Patents Act 1988.

Published by the Langley Press, 2023

To Miranda and Dan McGill

Joe Hill

Life and Death of an American Rebel

Simon Webb

Also from the Langley Press

John Lilburne: Gentleman, Leveller, Quaker

Jeremiah Dixon: Surveyor of the Mason-Dixon Line

1889-1895: The First Coronavirus Pandemic?

Pandemic Pieces

Lives of Famous Dwarfs

Absinthe Jack: Was Ernest Dowson Jack the Ripper?

For more from the Langley Press,
please visit our new website at
www.langleypress.co.uk

Contents

A Saturday Night in Salt Lake City   7

Mrs Hägglund's Boy   10

South of the Border   41

San Pedro   53

Under Arrest   58

On Trial   65

Outrage   75

The Songs   91

The Myth   101

Bibliography   109

A Saturday Night in Salt Lake City

After eleven-thirty at night on Saturday the tenth of January 1914 a tall, good-looking Swede turned up at the house of Doctor Frank McHugh in Salt Lake City, Utah. The man, who was then going by the name of Joe Hill, explained that he needed a doctor because, as he said in a husky voice, 'I've just been shot. I got into a stew with a friend of mine who thought I had insulted his wife. When he told me I had insulted his wife I knocked him down, but he got up and pulled a gun on me. I have walked away up here and I guess it isn't serious. Because this fellow that shot me didn't really know what he was doing, I want to have nothing said about it. If there's a chance to get over it, it will be OK with my friend.'

The physician and his wife welcomed Hill into their place on Fourteenth South and State Streets, which comprised their home and McHugh's surgery. The patient's shirt and under-shirt were soaked with blood, though there was no blood on, or bullet-holes in, Hill's light grey coat. At this point, the McHughs may have noticed that the bullet-hole in the front of their patient's knitted jacket, worn under the coat, was four inches lower than the hole in his chest.

Since Hill had walked to his house, McHugh may have been expecting to see a superficial wound, but he quickly realised that Joe had been shot in, or rather through, his chest. The bullet had entered the left side near the nipple, and exited at the back, leaving a ragged hole. McHugh was able to determine that the bullet had grazed Hill's left lung, which was bleeding slightly.

Seeing a light in the McHughs' window, another local medic, Dr A.A. Bird, decided to pop in for a visit. He arrived in time to see his friend McHugh dressing the stranger's wound, and helping him back into his clothes. During this process, a shoulder-holster with a pistol in it fell onto the floor. Dr McHugh put this into the pocket of his patient's coat. The physician decided that there was no point in sending Hill to the local hospital.

If the bullet had hit Joe Hill in the head, or the abdomen, or had entered his chest at a slightly different angle, the Swede might have died on the spot, or shortly after the shooting, or a few hours later in hospital. If the bullet had not torn right through his wiry frame he would have needed surgery to remove it.

Surgery, or at least a long period of bed-rest, would also have been required if the bullet had hit Hill's scapula or shoulder-blade (which it missed entirely), cracked a rib or pierced, rather than grazed, a lung. If the pistol that did the damage had been a larger-calibre weapon, or had been discharged closer to the victim, the Swede's story might have ended very differently.

As it was, Hill had been very lucky; and not for the first time. He had been lucky enough to survive a poverty-stricken childhood in Sweden, although three of his eight siblings had died as children. Back in Sweden, he had also survived tuberculosis, and the surgery and other treatments that had been tried to tackle the infection, in those days before antibiotics. During his new life in the United States, the lucky Swede had even survived at least one previous shooting, and the 1906 San Francisco earthquake and the raging fires that followed it, though thousands of others died. But soon after banging on Dr Frank McHugh's door in Salt Lake City, Utah, Joe Hill's luck started to run out.

Mrs Hägglund's Boy

Joe Hill, also known as Joseph Hillstrom, had been born Joel Emmanuel Hägglund on the seventh of October 1879 in the Swedish port city of Gävle (then spelled Gefle).

In the year of Joe Hill's birth, the United Kingdom, reigned over by the widowed Queen Victoria, began its war against the Zulus in Africa, and the American inventor Thomas Edison made one of his prototype electric light-bulbs burn for half a day. Henrik Ibsen's play *A Doll's House* premiered in Copenhagen, and Albert Einstein was born at Ulm in Germany.

Also in 1879 August Strindberg published *The Red Room*, thought to be the first modern Swedish novel. The book attacked the hypocrisy and snobbery of the Swedish middle class, and also showed an awareness of the plight of ordinary working people like the Hägglunds. Ingvar Andersson quotes a revealing passage in his *History of Sweden*. Here an impoverished Stockholm carpenter offers an insight into his grim life, and the unrest such suffering might lead to:

I assure you, ladies, things are already unbearable. And a day will come when they will be even worse; but then – then we will descend from our slums with a roar like a waterfall . . . and you shall eat potatoes till your bellies are tight as drums . . .

As well as being perhaps the first modern novel in the Swedish language, *The Red Room* is also Strindberg's attempt to give some idea of the state of Sweden in the year it was published, which was also the year Joe Hill was born. The hero, Arvid Falk, abandons his job in the civil service because he is never given any work to do: he visits office after office where the officials are either inactive or absent. In attempting to become a writer, he falls into dire poverty, partly because his elder brother has cheated him of his inheritance. As a trainee parliamentary reporter, Falk witnesses much time-wasting in the Stockholm *Rikstag*. Here the king's representative, complete with antiquated three-cornered hat, receives a great deal of attention, whereas a speech about the plight of ordinary people is completely ignored: when the speech starts, everyone goes off to lunch.

Quite apart from its political content, *The Red Room* includes evocative descriptions of life in a coastal city in Sweden at the time:

Far below him lay the noisy, reawakening town; the steam cranes whirred in the harbour, the iron bars rattled in the iron weighing machine, the whistles of the lock-keepers shrilled, the steamers at the pontoon bridge smoked, the omnibuses rumbled over the uneven paving-stones; noise and uproar in the fish market, sails and flags on the water outside; the screams of the sea-gulls, bugle-calls from the dockyard, the turning out of the guard, the clattering of the wooden shoes of the working-men . . .

(trans. Schleussner, 1913)

11

Outside Sweden, Strindberg is better known as a playwright than a novelist. His *Miss Julie* (1888) has become part of the standard theatrical repertoire all over the world, and there are many film and TV adaptations in English alone.

In February 1879, just a few months before Joe Hill was born, an aristocratic British politician with the improbable name Sir Mountstuart Elphinstone Grant Duff enjoyed a very interesting lunch at the Devonshire Club in London. One of his companions at the meal, which took a leisurely three hours, was 'a short, rather small' German 'with grey hair and beard which contrasts strangely with a still dark moustache'. Grant Duff found the man's conversation learned and dryly humorous, 'very *positif*, slightly cynical': overall, he was impressed, and remarked that he 'would gladly meet him again'.

The man was Karl Marx, who turned sixty-one in 1879, and by then had already been living in London for thirty years. He was already in the last home he would ever know, number forty-one Maitland Park Road, Hampstead. There he would die four years later, a little over a year after the death of his long-suffering wife, Jenny, and two months after the death of his favourite daughter. That Grant Duff thought Marx small is interesting, especially since in earlier years many were impressed by Karl's thick-set, powerful body. It seems that by 1879 the author of *Capital* was already suffering from the 'cachexy' or wasting away that was given as the cause of his death in 1883.

Although Marx's ideas would have a profound effect on left-wing thinking for decades, his were not the only notions then available to critics of the capitalist system. The Russian

Mikhail Bakunin (1814-1876) was a man of the Left like Marx, but came to believe that Marx's idea of the workers seizing power and bringing in the era of the 'dictatorship of the proletariat' would just mean the replacement of one form of tyranny with another. Bakunin and his followers were anarchists, who thought that the revolution that was sorely needed should not be imposed from above, but should emerge as the workers reorganised their workplaces and their communities into utopian cooperatives. Many of Bakunin's ideas, and those of his friend the French anarchist Pierre-Joseph Proudhon, influenced the Industrial Workers of the World (IWW) an organisation which Joe Hill joined in America around 1910.

One idea of Marx's that is surely relevant to the lives of active IWW members like Hill is his concept of the *alienation* of workers. Forced to produce goods that they could not personally own, in workplaces where their opinions counted for nothing, and feeling completely powerless, workers could feel utterly disconnected from their work roles. This feeling is reflected in the IWW assertion, enshrined in their constitution, which states that employers and employees have nothing in common.

In the utopia promised by groups like the IWW, workers could make a contribution to the production process that went beyond just tightening a succession of identical screws over and over again for hours every day. The IWW also wanted to see workers adequately recompensed for their time and effort, and they fought to reduce hours, improve safety and get children out of the workplace altogether, and into schools.

The Hägglund family home, a single-storey building with attic rooms, still stands in Gävle's old town. Since 2011 it has

13

housed a small museum, the Joe Hill-gården, which combines a re-creation of how the place must have looked in Hill's time, with a shop, and displays relating to Hill's achievements and influence. In summer the garden at the back hosts social and cultural events. The house seems to be a decent size, until one remembers that the Hägglunds were a family of eleven. Built out of wood, it must also have been something of a fire-trap, back in the days of open fires, candles and oil-lamps. In fact a huge fire devastated the city ten years before Joel Hägglund was born: he was to witness something similar during the aftermath of the San Francisco earthquake of 1906.

A professional photo of Joel's mother Margareta Catharina with six of her children shows typically pale, blonde Swedish youngsters, all with recently-trimmed hair and wearing their Sunday best. For the five boys in the picture, Sunday best consists of dark stockings and knee-breeches with dark jackets and snowy white collars. Joel himself is the thinnest of them: he looks watchful, suspicious and ready to respond in kind to any insult or injury.

A portrait photograph of Hill's father Olof shows where his famous son got his good looks. In his railway-conductor's cap and thick dark beard, Dad looks more like a handsome trawler captain than an official in a railway company.

Though poor, the family still managed to be very musical. Olof built a home organ which they all learned to play, and Joe could also sing, play the piano, accordion and guitar, and make up songs. His favourite instrument was the violin, which he was happy to play for hours on end without a break. Hill's home town of Gävle is still noted for its musical life. It has its own symphony orchestra and concert hall, and various musical people were born there, including the noted operatic soprano

Anna Bartels (1869-1950) and Ingrid Wickman, the mother of the American musician Yusuf Islam, previously known as Cat Stevens. In fact Yusuf, originally named Steven Geogiou, lived in Gävle for a while during his childhood.

The list of other notable people born in the same year as Joe Hill includes the Russian revolutionary Leon Trotsky (born Lev Bronstein) and the Swiss artist Paul Klee. Archduke Franz Ferdinand of Austria, whose assassination in 1914 would spark the First World War, was only six years older than Joe Hill; Gavrilo Prinsep, the archduke's assassin, was not born until 1894. In the United States in 1879, the White House was occupied by the largely forgotten nineteenth president, Rutherford B. Hayes, and in Hill's native Sweden the bewhiskered, capable, active and ambitious King Oscar III presided over a rapidly industrialising country with a growing population.

Sweden's industrialisation brought industrial unrest, and in the year Joel Hägglund, the future union activist, was born, the Swedes experienced their first major strike. This was among sawmill workers at Sundsvall, a coastal town like Gävle, but about one hundred and thirty miles further north than Hill's birthplace. Timber exports had been one of the first triggers of industrialisation in Sweden. The workers at Sundsvall went on strike because their wages had been decreased. There were about five thousand strikers, from more than twenty sawmills. The governor of Medelpad, the province in which Sundsvall lies, called in the troops, broke up the strike and forced the strikers to return to work. The sense of frustration and hopelessness that this provoked caused hundreds of the locals to emigrate to America in the next few years.

At first the Swedish unions had little interest in politics, but in 1886 the Stockholm unions adopted socialism. In the previous year a socialist newspaper called *The Social Democrat* started publishing, edited at first by August Teodor Palm (1879-1922). Palm was a political activist and trade union advocate who had delivered the first know socialist speech in Swedish history, in Malmö in 1881. Palm's life resembled Hill's in many respects. Both came from humble origins, both fought for unions and left-wing politics, both were well-travelled writers, and both suffered periods of imprisonment. While Hill worked in various low-skilled or unskilled jobs, relying on his formidable physical strength and stamina, Palm worked as a tailor.

August Palm was orphaned at the age of ten, and at eight Joe Hill, or Joel Hägglund, lost his father Olof. Dad had been injured at work, and he died in 1887 during an operation to stem internal bleeding.

Joel, his mother and his eight siblings had been poor even when Olof was alive, and they now found themselves experiencing truly dire poverty. Joel was forced to take work in a rope factory, and later as a stoker on a steam-powered crane.

Tuberculosis was the scourge of nineteenth-century families, and it is hardly surprising that Joel was afflicted with it as a young man in Sweden. 'TB' usually conjures up images of people suffering from the common pulmonary type, which affects the lungs. But the TB bacillus can attack other parts of the body, including bones and skin. Joel's case led to joint problems and lesions on his face and neck, which in those days, before antibiotics, could only be treated with x-rays or surgery. The x-ray treatment failed, and Joel's skin-lesions had to be cut off. This left him with an unusually thin nose, and some facial scarring.

Joel's mother was no stranger to surgical operations, and she endured no fewer than nine in the eighteen months before her death in January 1902. Her six surviving children decided to sell the old family home and divide the proceeds between them. With their shares, Joel and his brother Paul bought tickets on Cunard's transatlantic steamer *Saxonia*, planning to make new lives for themselves in America. Both had pretty good English, having learned it in classes organised by the Swedish YMCA. Joel may also have picked up the language while working on British-flagged ships sailing between Sweden and the British Isles. As a Germanic language, Swedish is not unlike English, so for Joel and Paul the language barrier would not have been as difficult as it would have been for immigrants from some places, where the people used a different alphabet, and spoke a language where none of the words resembled English words.

Paul and Joel were not leaving during the peak time of emigration from Sweden to the US, which had been around fifteen years earlier. In 1887, a record year, over three hundred and forty thousand Swedes had emigrated to the United States: in the first decade of the twentieth century, the average per year was nearer twenty thousand, a little more than a twentieth of what it had been when Joe Hill was a small boy. By the early years of the twentieth century, significant numbers of ex-pat Swedes were also returning to the home country from America. Many of the hopeful emigrants making the initial journey west would have started the first leg of their trip at the port of Gävle, where the Hägglunds had made their home.

Emigrants tearfully saying goodbye to friends and relatives on the docks at Gävle may have been a sight with which the Hägglunds were very familiar. There were also friends and relatives of the Hägglunds themselves among them. Joel and his family may also have been aware that Swedish settlement in America went back to at least the seventeenth century: the colony of New Sweden was founded in Delaware in 1638. Unfortunately the Dutch seized the settlement, named Fort Christina after the then queen of Sweden, in 1655.

In the US in the nineteenth and twentieth centuries, many white Swedish immigrants had the advantage of looking decidedly north European. They were unlikely to experience the prejudice directed by some whites against Black people, and others from southern Europe, where the people tend to be darker than they are in the north. Swedes could pass themselves off as WASPs – white Anglo-Saxon Protestants; although this acronym describing the historically least-disadvantaged group in American society did not come into use until the nineteen-sixties.

Some Swedes emigrated to avoid religious intolerance at home. The United States was meant to be the home of complete freedom of religion, where there would never be a state church. A feature of Swedish life in the nineteenth century was the growth of small churches that were independent of the Lutheran Church of Sweden, which continued to be the state church until the year 2000. The Hägglunds were members of the Waldenströmmare sect, an offshoot of Lutheranism that was inspired by the theological ideas of Paul Petter Waldenström (1838-1917). Waldenström might even have been a familiar figure to members of Joel's family – he taught at a school in Gävle from 1874 to 1905, and often preached at the old Bethlehem church there. The pulpit he used is preserved in the new Bethlehem church, which was built in 1986. A plaque in the new place commemorates Waldenström, and reads in part 'he gave our people a purer picture of God'.

Waldenström got himself noticed at a national level by publishing a popular novel, called *Squire Adamsson*, and going public with some unconventional theological ideas. Though many in the established church thought them scandalous, Waldenström's religious views could be thought of as an intensification of some familiar Protestant and Lutheran themes: the importance of one's own inner relationship with God, an emphasis on personal revelation and heart-felt conversion, the struggle to live a virtuous life, and a less marked reliance on church ceremonies and the priesthood.

The author of *Squire Adamsson* viewed the presence of Jesus in the universe as a great and divine gift to all the people of the world. His approach seemed to be particularly well-suited to the business of persuading doubters to make a real spiritual commitment, and Waldenström's sermons and writings were popular with the Swedes at home, and among Swedish expatriates in America and elsewhere. As a politician as well as a writer and a clergyman, Waldenström became a very influential figure. In his book *The Religious Origins of Democratic Pluralism*, published in 2016, Mark Safstrom suggested that Waldenström helped to guide Swedes to a new tolerance of differences of political opinion, partly by introducing them to new religious ideas.

It is tempting to speculate about the effect Joe Hill's religious upbringing might have had on his later life. As an enthusiastic participant in church get-togethers, he would certainly have learned how music could inspire people, and unite them. That his family followed the Waldenströmmare way may also have accustomed Hill to the business of being part of a minority of which others disapproved. Time among the followers of Waldenström may also have taught him the importance of working things out for himself, and trying to live a worthwhile life.

Hill's willingness to sacrifice himself for a great cause is echoed strangely in a letter from Carl Olof Rosenius (1816-1868), a mentor of Waldenström, quoted in translation in Saftstrom's 2015 selection of writings from the Swedish Pietists, the group with which Waldenström was most closely associated. Rosenius wrote that even if it meant working with preachers from different denominations, he was eager to 'offer my life, my strength for Christ and his commands . . . for the one holy universal church'.

Swedish families like the Hägglunds may have been attracted to new religious ideas and organisations because the old Church of Sweden was part of the structure of a society that seemed hide-bound, hierarchical and bureaucratic. Surely the king wielded too much power in a state that was supposed to be democratic, and year after year parliament failed to debate matters of daily importance to ordinary Swedes. This is hardly surprising – when Joel Hägglund left for America, only rich men (and no women) could vote, which meant that a mere eight percent of the population could express their wishes through the ballot-box.

Andersson's Swedish history has an interesting quotation that reveals what many Swedish emigrants were trying to get away from in the old country, and what they hoped to find in the new. Evidently the ex-pat who penned the letter from which Andersson quotes had not been disappointed by the New World. He asserts that he misses Sweden 'but little', and remembers 'the oppression of her less fortunate citizens . . . the undue power of the higher classes, the disregard and harshness with which they used to oppress the poor'. The unnamed writer goes on to assert that in America he had found 'a free land where all men have equal right to the benefits bestowed by the Creator – this is what I have sought, and found indeed'.

The egalitarian America that this letter writer had 'found indeed' would have been unrecognisable to many newcomers at the start of the twentieth century, and to millions who had been born in the United States. There were obscene inequalities of opportunity, education, wealth and power, and the situation for newcomers in particular was made worse by prejudice against 'foreigners', especially those who were racially different from the white ruling class.

In the southern states in particular, so-called 'Jim Crow' laws enforced segregation of Black and white people. Named after a nasty, caricatured idea of a Black man, Jim Crow laws merely reinforced disadvantage and discrimination. Even Black people with highly-valued skills would find themselves excluded from worthwhile employment, or paid less than their white equivalents when they found work.

Meanwhile many jobs were being de-skilled because of automation. Products that could previously only be made by highly-trained craftspeople were now being turned out faster, cheaper and sometimes better in more automated factories employing cheap unskilled labour. These workers were often drawn from the most disadvantaged and vulnerable segments of society, and they were easily fired and replaced. A particular concern at the beginning of the twentieth century was the way that employers were joining together into 'trusts', organisations with far more power than individual, locally-based concerns.

One response to the general situation was presented at a meeting at Brand's Hall in Chicago in June 1905, by which time Joe Hill had been in America for around three years. The meeting comprised nearly two hundred delegates, including representatives of socialist, anarchist and radical union organisations. What they achieved was the foundation of a new type of union, the Industrial Workers of the World, or IWW, the members of which eventually became known as 'Wobblies'. The nick-name is likeable, but it may not be ideal for an organisation that is supposed to stand firm against both the power of the employers and the system of capitalism itself.

One story of how the Wobblies got their nick-name is re-told by Franklin Rosemont in his book *Joe Hill: The IWW & the Making of a Revolutionary Workingclass Counterculture*. Rosemont quotes from an article on the subject published in *The Nation* magazine in 1923. The author, Mortimer Downing, related that back in 1911 the owner of a Chinese restaurant in Vancouver, Canada got into the habit of giving unlimited credit to hungry members of the IWW. When he asked customers if they were from the IWW, he pronounced 'W' as 'wobble'. Rosemont doubts if this is strictly accurate – it may be too good a story to be true – but it was nevertheless told and re-told among Wobblies for decades.

There were unions in America before the founding of the IWW, but these were generally 'trade' or 'craft' unions organised to protect the interests of specific categories of workers, many of whom were already in possession of valuable skills. Shockingly, many of these unions had an official policy of excluding women, and Black workers, however skilled they happened to be. Since their members were perceived to be doing well within the existing capitalist system, the old trade unions were often quite happy about the prospect of this system continuing.

The idea of reaching out to workers of both sexes and of every colour, nationality and language-group made the IWW seem very advanced and enlightened, and indeed they were up for some big challenges. In 1893, in a letter to his friend F.A. Sorge, Karl Marx's friend and collaborator Friedrich Engels had identified the diversity of the American workforce as a barrier to the organisation of any effective socialist political party in America. Engels noted how the distinction between native-born Americans and immigrants tended to divide the workers, as did their different races and national groups: Czech, Polish, Italian, Scandinavian, etc.

An approach devoid of racism seemed to be deep-rooted in the character of Bill Haywood, one of the IWW founders. Haywood had been born in Salt Lake City, the town that was to prove fatal to Joe Hill many years later. Growing up in the city, he had witnessed the lynching of a Black man by a mob who acted as arresting officer, judge, jury and executioner. He had also been appalled to witness the verbal humiliation of a Black man who had been part of the audience of a lecture given by a racist speaker.

In mining camps and various other places in the West, where Haywood worked and strove to organise his fellow-workers, the future Wobbly chief made friends with people of various ethnic groups. He had a particular admiration for Native Americans, and, in his autobiography, he went out of his way to bust the stereotypes about the First Nations people that were entertained by many immigrant groups. As a young man in the West, he had sought out older Native Americans and listened to their side of what had happened during the Indian Wars.

The colour-blindness that characterised the Wobblies' all-inclusive approach was personified in the career of Ben Fletcher (1890-1949), a leading Black Wobbly who helped organise the longshoremen (called 'dockers', 'dock-workers' or 'stevedores' in England) working in the port of Philadelphia. Fletcher's parents had been born in the 1850s, his father in Virginia and his mother in either Virginia or Maryland. It is likely that both of them had been born into slavery, but that they were freed when slavery was abolished throughout the US in 1865. They moved north to Philadelphia some thirty years before the 'official' start of the Great Migration, when from around 1910 some six million Black southerners moved north over the Mason-Dixon Line to avoid the Jim Crow laws in the South.

The Fletchers and their children found that discrimination and disadvantage were still serious threats to Black people in the North. Despite Philadelphia's reputation as the Quaker-founded 'city of brotherly love', Black workers struggled to find worthwhile work in the town, and, as elsewhere in the States, they were excluded from unions.

The irony is that though Fletcher's family had probably been living in North America for generations, and were therefore far more American than a Swedish newcomer like Joel Hägglund, Joe's white skin gained him far more acceptance in his new country than a US-born Black man could expect. Fletcher's credentials as a true American may have been even more impressive: he may have had Native American blood. Benjamin Harrison Fletcher was even named after the American president who was in office when he was born: Benjamin Harrison (1833-1901; president 1889-1893).

Because the IWW did not exclude Black people from membership, Ben Fletcher was able to join in 1910, at the age of twenty, the same year Joe Hill may have joined, though the latter turned thirty-one that year. Fletcher contributed articles to Wobbly newspapers, and soon emerged as an inspiring leader and an interesting, amusing and persuasive public speaker. It is likely that Joe Hill did not possess anything like Fletcher's oratorical gifts: it seems that in a hall full of Wobblies, Ben would make for the podium, while Joe would head for the piano.

Like Joe's, there are many holes in Fletcher's life-story as it has been passed down to us. His biographer Peter Cole puts this down to the tendency of the lives of ordinary workers, and even extraordinary workers, to vanish into the mists of history. Cole also mentions lost IWW documentation, some of it deliberately destroyed by the US government. This paucity of material means that Cole's biography of the great Black Wobbly, printed at the front of his book, is necessarily very short, but still includes a lot of speculation about where Ben was and when, and what he might have been doing, and the role he might have played in various events.

Cole reports what happened on the docks and among the dock-workers when Ben was certainly present in Philadelphia, but the scarcity of hard information means that the author sometimes has to resort to guessing that Fletcher may have been central to events, but chose to keep a low profile. What happened was not that a union persuaded the longshoremen to strike, but that in 1913 the longshoremen struck and were then persuaded to join the IWW.

The IWW was well-suited to the task of organising a workforce of this type: the longshoremen were ethnically diverse, and they may not all have got a fair crack of the whip in another union that did not have anti-racist ideas written into its DNA. The 1910 census revealed that about twenty-six percent of Philadelphia longshoremen were white and had been born in the US, twenty-seven percent had been born outside of the States, and over forty percent were Black Americans.

In 1913 Joe Hill wrote one of his most popular songs: *There is Power in a Union*:

> There is pow'r there is pow'r in a band of workingmen,
> When they stand hand in hand,
> That's a pow'r, that's a pow'r
> That must rule in every land—
> One Industrial Union Grand.

Along the docks in Philadelphia, after the strike of 1913 and the subsequent unionisation of the longshoremen, a lot of power was wrested from the employers and placed in the hands of leading local Wobblies like Ben Fletcher. They rearranged things so that the employers now had to ask the union to deploy workers for them, and they kept non-IWW longshoremen off the docks altogether. The Wobblies also abolished the divisive practice of arranging the longshoremen into work-gangs according to ethnicity. Now everyone worked together.

The later pages of Cole's book on Fletcher, a second edition of which appeared in 2020, include a lot of primary source material in the form of articles and speeches: these are what Fletcher left behind in lieu of detailed information about all of his activities; while Joe Hill left songs, cartoons, letters and journalism.

As well as trying to represent and help both skilled and unskilled workers regardless of skin-colour, the IWW wanted to use industrial and political action to overthrow and replace capitalism itself. Their alternative would be a system of production run by and for the workers: the Wobblies were therefore 'syndicalists'. Although they undoubtedly shared some ideas with the Marxists of the time, and two eminent early Wobs even died in Soviet Russia, the IWW was never intended to be a political party, and its political ideas were closer to those of anarchists and anarcho-syndicalists, including such figures as the aforementioned French philosopher Pierre-Joseph Proudhon, and the Russian Mikhail Bakunin.

In the words of William D. Haywood, in the first address to what he called 'the Continental Congress of the Working Class' in 1905, the delegates were in Chicago to help create 'a working-class movement in possession of the economic powers, the means of life, in control of the machinery of production and distribution without regard to capitalist masters'.

The philosophy of the IWW was nicely summed up in the preamble to the Wobbly constitution, as agreed in 1905. The Preamble, a version of which is still cherished by the Wobblies, declared that 'there can be no peace' while the 'employing class' had 'all the good things of life' while the workers experienced 'hunger and want'. Without 'affiliation with any political party' workers were to 'take and hold that which they produce by their labour'.

English readers might find that the Wobblies' determination to seize control of the means of production is reminiscent of the iconic Clause Four of the constitution of the British Labour party, which was first introduced in 1918. For years this was printed on the back of Labour party membership cards, until it was replaced under party leader Tony Blair in 1995. The old Clause Four advocated securing for the workers 'the full fruits of their industry . . . upon the basis of the common ownership of the means of production, distribution and exchange'.

'Big Bill' Haywood's use of the phrase 'Continental Congress' during that founding meeting in Chicago in 1905 was a pointed reference to the so-called Continental Congresses of the eighteenth century in America, one of which came up with the Declaration of Independence in 1776. The implication was that this new 'Continental Congress of the Working Class' would also be revolutionary, and kick the capitalists out of American industry, just as George Washington and the other rebels had kicked the British out of what became the United States.

In the British context, 'common ownership of the means of production, distribution and exchange' has tended to mean the nationalisation of businesses, services and sometimes whole industries. To put it very simply, nationalisation usually means that the the business, service or industry comes to be owned by all the people and run by the government. This is not exactly what the Wobblies wanted back in Chicago in 1905. What they envisaged was more like a network of workers' cooperatives where, it would seem, the distinction between union shop-stewards and managers would become meaningless.

A particular grievance of the first Wobblies, as mentioned in the Preamble, was 'the centring of the management of industries into fewer and fewer hands' which, they believed, led to 'the ever-growing power of the employing class'. The only thing that could counter this power was 'an organization formed in such a way that all its members in any one industry, or in all industries, if necessary, cease work whenever a strike or lockout is on in any department thereof, thus making an injury to one an injury to all'.

'An injury to one is an injury to all' is a slogan still used by the Wobblies, but the version of the Preamble included on the current UK IWW website includes more about the abolition of the wage system and, in the adapted second paragraph, an environmental message:

Between these two classes a struggle must go on until the workers of the world organise as a class, take possession of the means of production, abolish the wage system, and live in harmony with the Earth.

Manifestos, constitutions and their preambles, which are often written by committees and couched in cautious legalese, can make for very dry reading. From the start, the Wobblies were adept at putting their message across in ways that were accessible to the kind of people who did not regard an afternoon poring over Marx's *Capital* as a fun time. The IWW used leaflets, postcards, fiction, poetry, stickers and cartoons to promote the cause, and soon Wobbly songs began to appear. This was the field in which Joe Hill particularly distinguished himself.

The Wobblies' determination to embrace even the most disadvantaged workers included in particular the tens of thousands of so-called 'hoboes' who were a feature of American life in the early twentieth century, especially in the West. For years, Joe Hill lived as a hobo; a homeless itinerant worker who drifted around in search of employment. Hoboes travelled thousands of miles by hopping on and off the long, slow freight-trains that rumbled constantly throughout the land. Since the hoboes paid no fares, this mode of transport was illegal as well as dangerous. If they couldn't get on a train, hoboes would walk the tracks, as these sometimes led to destinations no roads had yet reached. In many cases, the tracks themselves had been laid by fellow hoboes.

It was estimated that at any one time, there might have been half a million drifters riding trains, waiting for trains or walking the tracks. During Joe Hill's early years in the US, perhaps as many as ten thousand a year were killed or injured trying to get free rides. If accidents didn't hurt the hoboes, the railway police might, or the train guards. The jobs the members of this huge floating population were looking for were usually temporary or seasonal, and involved hard physical work. They worked in logging camps, sawmills and canning factories. Many followed the harvest north, gathering in corn, fruit and vegetables.

On the job, hoboes sometimes lived in accommodation provided by their employers – often filthy, lice-infested bunk-houses. They ate the frequently poor and inadequate food from the works canteen, or were forced to buy their food, and everything else, from overpriced shops linked to the company. Money was deducted from their pay for their food and accommodation, and for inadequate and sometimes non-existent medical cover.

To get at employment at all, the ladies and gentlemen of the road often had to go through crooked employment agents, who would charge them to register. The employment agents were sometimes in league with the employers, or whoever was responsible for hiring and firing at particular employer's premises. These people took a cut of the employment agents' fees, so that there was an incentive to hire a steady stream of new workers, making the jobs in question even less secure. The moral of this story is that however poor you are, there will always be someone ready to try to extract money out of you.

Between jobs, hoboes lived in skid-row rented rooms or the so-called 'hobo jungles', informal settlements at the edge of town, where tents and other demountable homes were arranged around a big fire where 'mulligans', all-inclusive stews, were cooked. In the depression years of the thirties, these shanty-towns would become known as 'Hoovervilles' after Herbert Hoover, the US president whose dogmatic policies only seemed to make the national situation worse.

It is hardly surprising that those who were forced to live this desperate type of live were tempted to drink too much, when they got the chance, and to use cheap prostitutes.

The IWW was keen to embrace the denizens of the hobo jungles, who had long been neglected by traditional trade unions and pretty much everyone else. Wobbly ideas, and particularly the songs the group produced, were popular among the hoboes, and soon the IWW became associated in the popular imagination with this unfortunate section of the American population. Wobbly songs, such as those devised by Joe Hill, were sung in the hobo jungles. IWW ideas and literature would circulate, and Wobbly offices offered members somewhere to go when they arrived in a new town. Members lucky enough to have their own homes might also offer hospitality to those who were less fortunate.

Joe Hill spent many years as a wandering hobo, but from 1910, when he joined the IWW in San Pedro, California, the Swede was a union man as well as an itinerant labourer. Researching his pioneering biography of Joe, published in 1969, Gibbs Smith had great difficulty working out exactly where Hill was during his years as a drifter, which is hardly surprising. Joe and his fellow hoboes were deliberately living off-grid (as we would say today), being paid cash-in-hand and in some cases lying about their names, where they had come from and where they were going.

Gibbs Smith included a lot of places Hill might have been, and things he might have done, but his summary of what he believed his subject had definitely been doing during this mysterious period amounted to a scant one hundred and nineteen words.

Naturally taciturn, Hill gave out minimal and contradictory hints as to his movements from 1902, when he first arrived in America, and 1914, when he was arrested in Salt Lake City. That his name morphed from Joel Hägglund to Joseph Hillstrom to Joe Hill during this time may have something to do with a desire to cover his tracks, and to skirt round black-listing: employers would share lists of workers likely to cause union trouble, so a change of name could be advisable.

Joe may have lived and worked in New York for a year or so after landing in that city in 1902. Here he may have been employed for a time as a porter in a bar in the Bowery area. He may then have moved on to Chicago, where he was fired from a job in a machine shop because he was attempting to organise a union, although he would not yet have been a member of the IWW at that time. He may then have drifted through various other places including Philadelphia, the Dakotas, Spokane in Washington State, Cleveland, Ohio, and Portland, Oregon. Hill's time in San Pedro, Los Angeles, immediately before his fateful trip to Salt Lake City in 1914, is well-attested.

We know that Hill was in San Francisco at the time of the 1906 earthquake because his account of the quake was published in a Gävle newspaper, the *Gefle Dägblad*, in May of that year. Joe was woken by the shaking early in the morning of April the eighteenth, and was lucky to get out of the building alive. He fell right through some collapsing stairs into a basement, from which he managed to emerge with nothing worse than a few bruises.

Outside, he saw wide cracks in the pavement, collapsed or semi-collapsed buildings, and the beginnings of the fire that would soon tear through the city. He was given an axe and a helmet and pressed into service as a fireman, helping to evacuate people from burning buildings. Martial law was imposed, and Hill remarked in his article that if he had attempted to loot anything, he would have been shot. At this time, when the population should have been pulling together, the shortage of food tempted some into profiteering. A grocer who was selling crackers for twenty times their usual price was tied to a pole in the street, and the police encouraged people to spit on him.

In 1911, Hill spent some time living in a shack on the beach at Hilo, Hawaii with fellow-Wobbly Harry 'Mac' McClintock. McClintock, also known as 'Haywire Mac', was an IWW activist and songwriter like Joe himself. He wrote the song *Halleluja, I'm a Bum* about the hobo life, in which the lyrics state that if you live as a bum, 'Your home is always near; | The moon's your chandelier'. In 1928, Haywire Mac recorded his biggest hit, *The Big Rock Candy Mountain*, a whimsical piece about a sort of hobo paradise where:

All the cops have wooden legs
And the bulldogs all have rubber teeth
And the hens lay soft-boiled eggs

The song was used with great effect in the surreal 2000 film *Oh Brother, Where Art Thou?*, set during the Depression era and directed by the Coen brothers. Haywire Mac was also recorded singing and playing (on the guitar) Joe Hill's song *The Preacher and the Slave*. Since no recordings of Joe Hill survive (and indeed none may have been made in the first place) this archive recording by a man who had lived with Hill may be the closest we can get to the authentic Joe Hill sound.

At Hilo, Hill and Haywire Mac were employed loading raw sugar onto boats for export to the United States (Hawaii was not a state at the time). It is surely significant that many of the locations where Joe Hill lived and worked, including Hilo, San Francisco and San Pedro were ports. These places may have reminded the ex-pat Swede of his home town of Gävle, and it is likely that he knew the kinds of work that could be found in a port, and had enough experience of and expertise in such work to be able to hold on to a job in such a place. Even the town of Yale, British Columbia, where Hill popped up during a strike by railway construction workers in 1912, is a port on the Fraser River. It was here that Hill wrote his song *Where the Fraser River Flows*:

Where the Fraser river flows, each fellow worker knows,

They have bullied and oppressed us, but still our union grows.

And we're going to find a way, boys, for shorter hours and better pay, boys

And we're going to win the day, boys, where the Fraser river flows.

Joe Hill's birthplace (Anna Sanvaresa)

Bill Haywood

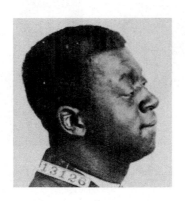

Ben Fletcher

Joe Hill plaque in San Pedro, California (Eugene Daub)

Ricardo and Enrique Flores Magón

Elizabeth Gurley Flynn

President Woodrow Wilson

Swedish commemorative stamp (Anna Sanvaresa)

Helen Keller

Swedish train named for Joe Hill (Anna Sanvaresa)

South of the Border

Like many of the workers who were attracted to the IWW, Hill could turn his hand to practically anything, and it seems that in 1911, the year before his trip to Canada, he turned his hand to soldiering.

We have seen how, in the early years of the twentieth century, the governments of the United States and of Joe's native Sweden neglected the struggles and aspirations of many of their citizens. In both countries this led to violence and unrest, but in Mexico it triggered waves of bloody revolution.

The Mexican president, Porfirio Díaz, had been in power, on and off, for over thirty years, and turned eighty in 1910, the year revolution came. Díaz loved to pose for photographs in magnificent military uniforms studded with medals, or sharp civilian suits, looking imperturbable behind his silvery handlebar moustache.

To stay in office, Díaz tweaked the constitution, rigged elections and silenced opposition voices. Troublesome newspapers would be suspended or shut down, their journalists thrown into prison or assassinated. By contrast, papers that supported the regime (some of which were set up by Díaz's cronies) received generous government subsidies.

Journalists critical of the Díaz regime certainly had plenty to write about. In the capital, Mexico City, it was possible to imagine that the country was rapidly modernising and industrialising in a way that was sure to benefit everyone, thanks in part to the wisdom of the so-called *Cientificos*, the coterie of technocrats who advised Díaz.

Outside of the capital, things did not look so rosy. Much of the industrialisation and modernisation had been brought by companies based in the US and elsewhere, who wanted to get their hands on Mexico's mineral wealth in particular. The benefits from their mining operations did not stick to everyone, and miners, often working in tough and dangerous conditions, were trying to unionise and push back.

One complaint of Mexican miners was that they were often paid far less than miners from the US who were doing exactly the same work. They were also subject to racial discrimination from white managers and fellow-workers, who referred to them as 'greasers'.

US interests in Mexico meant that many American citizens were making a lot of money off the backs of the poor Mexicans. The US newspapers had a tendency to idolise Díaz and his regime: north of the border it was believed that only 'the General' (as he was often called) could keep Mexico stable enough to keep the profits flowing. The millionaire newspaper proprietor William Randolph Hearst, who was the original for Charles Foster Kane in Orson Welles' 1941 film *Citizen Kane,* owned millions of acres of land in northern Mexico. Naturally none of his papers were going to pick holes in the General. At the time, Hearst's newspapers and magazines included the *San Francisco Daily Examiner*, the *New York Journal*, the *Los Angeles Examiner*, *Motor* magazine and *Cosmopolitan*. It is thought that these publications were read by over twenty million people.

Many big landowners who, unlike Hearst, were native to Mexico, also wanted to see Díaz continue in office. They often owned land that had once been farmed by the locals, but had been seized to add to spreading *haciendas*, large estates that could be highly profitable. In parts of the country, convicts were being used as slave labour; and 'peonage', a system of debt slavery, meant that some Mexicans were scarcely more free than the journalists the Díaz regime threw into prison.

Time spent as an inmate in Mexico City's notorious Belén jail often amounted to a death-sentence, even if the prisoner was not executed by firing-squad outdoors in the prison garden, as many were. Overcrowded and filthy, prisoners housed in the basement had to endure atrocious conditions. Their only toilets were holes in the floor, and the whole basement would sometimes flood, with appalling results. Typhus, also known as jail-fever, was endemic in this awful place, which had opened as a prison during Díaz's last long stint in office, from 1884 to 1911.

One of the journalists who languished in this twentieth-century dungeon was Ricardo Flores Magón (1874-1922). Like Díaz himself, Magón was from the Mexican state of Oaxaca, of which Díaz had been governor from 1880 to 1883. Both men were also Mestizos, meaning that they had mixed Spanish and Native American ancestry. With his dark hair, oval glasses and handlebar moustache, Ricardo looked for all the world like a Mexican version of his Russian contemporary, the revolutionary Leon Trotsky, who as we know was born in the same year as Joe Hill.

From 1900, Ricardo and his brothers Enrique and Jesús published *Regeneración*, a newspaper that was highly critical of the Díaz regime. Harassed by repeated imprisonments, the brothers fled to Texas in 1904, where they continued to publish *Regeneración* from San Antonio, though they were so hard up that they sometimes had to work as labourers to make ends meet.

Regeneración, which had English-language as well as Spanish content, served a worthy purpose in both Mexico and the United States because it tried to present a truthful picture of what was really happening south of the border, something that readers of English were not getting from US newspapers such as those owned by Hearst. Some idea of the desperation of ordinary Mexicans, especially those with Native American blood, can be gleaned from Jack London's tale *The Mexican*, published in 1911. Here Rivera, the young hero of the story, looks back on his childhood:

He saw the white-walled, water-power factories of Rio Blanco. He saw the six thousand workers, starved and wan, and the little children, seven and eight years of age, who toiled long shifts for ten cents a day. He saw the perambulating corpses, the ghastly death's heads of men who laboured in the dye-rooms. He remembered that he had heard his father call the dye-rooms the "suicide-holes," where a year was death.

Unfortunately Jack London's stance on Mexican affairs at the time was compromised by his essay *The Trouble Makers of Mexico* (1914), in which he suggested that Mexicans of mixed Spanish and Indian blood, like the Flores Magón brothers, were behaving 'like a family of small children playing with sticks of dynamite on the front porch, in the basement, and up in the attic of their dwelling'.

For readers of English, another source of information on Mexico were the writings of John Kenneth Turner, whose articles on America's neighbour to the south began appearing in the *American Magazine* in 1909. On a trip to Mexico in 1907, Turner had found, among other things, a system of slavery operating in the Valle Nacional. Here natives from the Yaqui group were sold to the local planters for sixty-five American dollars each. Turner's articles were compiled into a book called *Barbarous Mexico* in 1910. The book includes an interview with Ricardo Flores Magón that was conducted by Turner in a prison in Los Angeles in 1908.

North of the border, the Flores Magóns were closely watched by the US authorities, and President Díaz's agents were determined to track them down. In December 1904, an unknown assailant forced his way into Ricardo's home and tried to stab him to death. Ricardo's brother Enrique was able to restrain the man, but the Texas police responded by arresting Enrique and letting the attacker go. Thus began a series of wanderings for the Flores Magón brothers, their followers (the so-called 'Magonistas') and their newspaper, wanderings which could be compared to Joe Hill's wanderings throughout the United States and into Canada.

Ricardo in particular spent a lot of time in prison north of the Mexican border: sometimes he was locked up because he was known to be trying to influence the politics of his home country of Mexico, and this contravened the US neutrality laws of the time. During his years in the United States, Ricardo became increasingly political, or perhaps we should say that he felt more able to publicly exhibit his left-leaning, anarchist tendencies. In exile, the Flores Magón brothers founded a new Mexican political party, the PLM or *Partido Liberal Mexicano*. This was not a liberal party in the sense that most English speakers would understand today: it was anarchist and pro-revolution.

The manifesto of the new party was published in *Regeneración,* which became the official newspaper of the PLM. The brothers and their comrades now became the 'Junta'. Their radical stance lost them many friends in their homeland, including Francisco Madero, who became president of Mexico after the fall of Díaz in 1911. Madero, the son of a rich and powerful family, had loaned two thousand dollars to the publishers of *Regeneración* when they were based in San Antonio.

While Ricardo and his brothers lost friends south of the border, they gained friends, money and other help from left-wingers in the United States, including members of the IWW. The support was surely welcome, but many Mexicans, who distrusted the American 'gringos', wanted a revolution run by and for themselves. To some, the PLM's reliance on gringo soldiers looked like Mexican collaboration with an invasion from the US. Mexicans with long memories might have remembered the 1853 attempt to invade Mexico by the American adventurer William Walker (1824-1860).

Ricardo Flores Magón shared many ideas with those Wobblies who were interested in the theoretical basis of their organisation, which is surely one reason why the IWW offered him so much help. While some of the better-read Wobblies were anarcho-syndicalists in the tradition of Bakunin, Ricardo was enchanted with the ideas of the anarchist Russian prince,

Peter Kropotkin (1842-1921). Kropotkin's 1892 book *The Conquest of Bread*, regarded as an anarchist classic, served Magón as a substitute Bible: he distributed two thousand copies of a Spanish translation in Mexico City in 1902:

The result of this state of things is that all our production tends in a wrong direction. Enterprise takes no thought for the needs of the community. Its only aim is to increase the gains of the speculator. Hence the constant fluctuations of trade, the periodical industrial crises, each of which throws scores of thousands of workers on the streets.

In his *The Mexican*, which includes thinly-disguised characters and incidents based on the PLM's activities and leading personnel on the brink of the Mexican revolution of 1911, Jack London wrote that:

Once started, the Revolution would take care of itself. The whole Díaz machine would go down like a house of cards. The border was ready to rise. One Yankee, with a hundred IWW men, waited the word to cross over the border and begin the conquest of Lower California.

'Lower California' is also called Baja California: it is a narrow peninsular that runs along the coast of Mexico, separating the Gulf of California from the Pacific. Despite the name 'California', Baja California and the gulf it creates are both in Mexico, not in the US state of California. The aforementioned William Walker, who had attempted to invade Mexico with his private army in 1853, had proclaimed the independence of the spurious 'Republic of Baja California' in that year.

From a twenty-first century perspective, it is tempting to compare the participation of American leftists in the Mexican revolution of 1911 to the activities of the International Brigades in Spain during the Spanish Civil War, between 1936 and 1938. In fact a number of Wobblies from America and elsewhere fought and died in the war against the Spanish Nationalists, some of them joining anarchist or anarcho-syndicalist outfits such as the Durruti International Battalion and the Confederación Nacional del Trabajo (CNT).

Back in 1911, the PLM plan was to invade Baja California and use it as a base from which to take over an ever-increasing area of Mexico. If PLM-inspired troops suffered reversals, fighting from village to village, town to town and city to city, they could retreat to their stronghold on the peninsular, lick their wounds and regroup. From the start, the scheme was compromised because the rebels only managed to capture the northern part of the peninsular.

The invasion, or revolution, or whatever it was, started at the end of January 1911. There were perhaps five hundred Magonista fighters, of whom about a fifth were gringos. This makes Jack London's mention in his story *The Mexican* of 'a hundred IWW men' ring true. Although Joe Hill later denied any involvement, it is clear that both he, and perhaps fellow-Wobby Frank Little, fought for Magón.

If he did participate, Little's involvement is surprising given the Quaker element in his upbringing, and his active and vocal opposition to America's later involvement in the Great War. Frank continued to act as a Wobbly union agitator during this time, though he was then liable to fall foul of emergency powers Woodrow Wilson's administration had given itself, to suppress activity that might hinder the war-effort. In the event, Frank Little was lynched by masked vigilantes who hanged him from a bridge in Butte, Montana in the summer of 1917.

Little's murder makes him one of the IWW's martyrs. Whether Joe Hill can also be counted as such depends on whether he was framed for murder by the Utah authorities because of his union involvement, or whether he would have received the same treatment if he had never been a member of any union. That powerful people in Montana wanted Frank Little dead is close to certain. The author Dashiell Hammett was then working for the Pinkerton detective agency as a strike-breaker in Butte. He often repeated the story that he was offered five thousand dollars to murder Little.

Shortly before his execution in Salt Lake City in 1915, Joe Hill told his attorney that in 1911 he had heard of 'a mob' which had 'attempted to loot Tijuana from the American side' but that although he had 'been credited with having been a lieutenant of that mob . . . this is absolutely untrue. I was then in San Pedro and there heard of the affair'.

It is hard to accept Hill's denial when other Wobblies reported fighting with him there, and when his written account of part of his time as a gun-slinging revolutionary south of the border is also extant. In a 1913 article in the *Industrial Worker* magazine, Hill wrote about visitors from the US who would travel down to Baja California on Sundays to see 'the wild men with their red flag':

But if the Mexican or the Indian regiment happened to be a little overjoyed from drinking "mescal" and took a notion to have a bit of sociable target practice, or to try to make buttonholes for one another without taking their clothes off, then "the people" would almost break their legs to get to their stinkwagons and make a bee-line for the "Land of the Graft and the Home of the Slave."

This glimpse of Hill's days as a fighting Magonista when, as he said, 'the red flag was flying in Lower California' hints at some of the reasons why the flag only flew down there for about six months. The fact that there were distinct Mexican, Indian and white US elements to the army caused problems: in particular, the white men tended to ignore orders from their darker officers.

If it is true that Hill witnessed drunken local troops firing their weapons, then this would also seem to suggest a serious lack of discipline. Surely this wouldn't happen in a well-ordered military base or camp, where visiting civilians of any colour should be able to feel perfectly safe. Whatever the tendency of the locals to get drunk and trigger-happy, it is also possible that anarchist American hoboes don't make the most disciplined soldiers either.

Despite their alleged indiscipline, the rebels managed to capture the towns of Mexicali and Tijuana, then home to about four hundred people between them. In Tijuana, a town Hill mentioned in his 1915 denial of any participation, the Magonistas opened up the prison, released all the prisoners, and burned down the bull-ring. They also banned alcohol and gambling, and ordered any mere self-seeking mercenary soldiers to leave town.

Most of the three hundred or so inhabitants of Mexicali left the town after it fell to the rebels without a shot being fired. The rebels tried to organise the remaining citizens along lines inspired by Kropotkin's *Conquest of Bread*, Ricardo Flores Magón's favourite book. They built a free library which was also supposed to have educational facilities: in his *Conquest of Bread* the anarchist prince had used the example of free libraries to show how in his time some societies were already working towards a form of communism:

Museums, free libraries, free schools, free meals for children; parks and gardens open to all; streets paved and lighted, free to all; water supplied to every house without measure or stint - all such arrangements are founded on the principle: "Take what you need."

In his story *The Mexican*, Jack London tried to convey how his fictionalised revolutionaries pictured the imminent revolution:

The people would rise. The defences of city after city would crumple up. State after state would totter down. And at last, from every side, the victorious armies of the Revolution would close in on the City of Mexico itself, Diaz's last stronghold.

This is indeed what happened, except that, as we have seen, 'the people' who rose up were not a homogenous group, and the revolution's 'victorious armies' were not all fighting for the same future vision of Mexico.

The rebels had some success against regular Mexican troops, the *Federales*, loyal to Díaz, but according to a book on the revolution by Ethel Duffy Turner, the widow of John Kenneth Turner, it was an unsuccessful battle against these troops, in which Joe Hill participated, that convinced some of the Wobbly warriors that it was time to go home.

In her *Revolution in Baja California: Ricardo Flores Magón's High Noon* Turner reported how Hill joined a patrol tasked with trying to find the *Federales*. They located them a few miles south of Tijuana, and an engagement ensued during which one of the rebels was killed. The rest fled back to

Tijuana under a hail of machine-gun fire, and many, among them Joe Hill, slipped over the border into the US. This ignominious defeat may be why Hill later tried to deny his role in the whole business. Since he denied all involvement while under threat of execution in Utah in 1915, he may have been trying to distance himself from the Magonistas because he did not want the authorities in the Mormon state to think of him in his role of armed revolutionary.

Other white Magonistas successfully fought off troops loyal to Porfirio Díaz, but later faced 'Maderist' forces fighting for the new president-in-waiting, Francisco Madero. The Maderists regained control of Baja California, and, as related by Steve Devitt in *The Pen That Set Mexico on Fire*, his 2017 book on Ricardo Flores Magón, the remaining gringo rebels agreed to disobey Magón, lay down their weapons, accept ten dollars and return home, after they had been treated to a slap-up meal in a Chinese restaurant.

Things did not end so well for Ricardo Flores Magón. He was arrested under the US Espionage Act of 1917, supposedly designed to discourage people from hindering America's efforts to aid the Allies in the Great War. He died at Leavenworth Penitentiary in Kansas in 1922, at the age of forty-eight. Ricardo's great enemy, the dictator Porfirio Díaz, was rather luckier. He had died a free man in Paris in 1915, at the age of eighty-four.

San Pedro

Ethel Duffy Turner relates that in the Magonista camp in Tijuana Joe Hill had behaved pretty much as he usually did among his fellow-workers wherever he found them. He played his violin, sang his songs, drew cartoons and generally bolstered morale with his 'warm, agreeable yet quiet disposition'.

Back in San Pedro after his time in Canada where, as we know, he had visited strikers in Yale, British Columbia, Hill worked on his songs in the IWW hall and the Sailor's Rest Mission. John Makins, superintendent of the mission, tried to convert Hill to Christianity, or rather make him return to it and abandon the IWW. This didn't work, although, as Makins wrote, 'he used our piano a great deal, for he was a musician'.

Malgren's Hall in San Pedro, where Hill is supposed to have cooked up some of his songs, was also the metaphorical kitchen where the local Wobblies devised the menu for a strike of some local men. In July 1912 two hundred Italian dock-workers who were employed by the Banning Company on Crescent Wharf downed tools, demanding better pay and shorter hours. By this time, Joe Hill was the secretary of the local IWW, and although the strike ended after a few days, the San Pedro police continued to harass any Wobblies they could find. Hill claimed that having failed to deport him as a foreigner, the cops locked him up for thirty days as a vagrant. By contrast, the police claimed that he had been arrested as a suspect in a streetcar holdup (streetcars are called 'trams' in Britain) but had been released when nobody could identify him.

When he wasn't working, languishing in prison, or hanging around Malgren Hall or the Seaman's Mission, some of Joe Hill's time in San Pedro was spent in the local hobo jungle, called Happy Hollow. There he met two Swedish brothers, also dock-workers, Edward and John Eselius. He would meet the brothers again in Salt Lake City.

Since 2017, Joe Hill's time in San Pedro has been commemorated with an eight-foot wide bronze plaque, located in Liberty Hill Plaza. This shows Hill in shallow relief, wearing the hat, tipped well back on his head, that he wears in the best-known surviving photograph of him. The bronze Hill is playing a guitar and holding a small book, perhaps the Wobblies' celebrated *Little Red Songbook*. His head is haloed, as it were, with the logo of the IWW, and to his right is a scene of dock-workers confronting blackjack-wielding police. To his left are workers in a cage: below them is a scroll with words adapted from Hill's song *Workers of the World, Awaken*:

We workers take a notion,
We can stop all speeding trains;
Every ship upon the oceans
We can tie with mighty chains;
Every wheel in the creation,

Every mine and every mill,
Fleets and armies of all nations,
Will at our command stand still.

The plaque was designed by Suzanne Matsumiya, a graphic designer for *Random Lengths News*, an alternative newspaper based in LA. It was made by Eugene Daub, who also made the statue of civil rights heroine Rosa Parks, which now stands in the Capitol in Washington DC.

Visitors to this part of San Pedro who are not familiar with the story of Joe Hill's life might be forgiven for mistaking the subject of the plaque for a modern pop-star rather than a man who died in 1915. The gravel-voiced American actor/singer/song-writer Tom Waits springs to mind. He has the same spare build as Joe Hill had, and he is often pictured wearing a dark hat with a brim, pushed far back on his head. On stage as a singer, and on screen as an actor, Waits often seems to personify the eternal American hobo, cool but scruffy, a drifter, always in some sort of trouble with the law. The irony is that some singers and others who have assumed the destitute hobo persona, such as Waits, Bob Dylan and Willie Nelson, have become highly successful and very rich.

The Joe Hill plaque in San Pedro was partly funded by contributions from retired dock-workers of the International Longshore and Warehouse Union (ILWU). The unveiling happened during Donald Trump's presidency, and the historian Vivian Price, speaking at the event, asserted that:

Now we have an administration that's trying to stop the right to organize . . . we have to know the past. We have to celebrate our heroes, and then find the heroes among us who are courageous and willing to speak up today.

David Arian, a past president of the local ILWU, added:

This plaque now becomes part of that progressive history that we can remind America of over and over again. This is who we are; this is the real America, not Trump's America.

Despite attempts to install some sort of memorial to Joe Hill in the Salt Lake City park where his prison used to be, the San Pedro plaque remains Hill's only monument in the US. Today, the plaque has to be viewed against the background of statues and other monuments that have been removed or defaced in the years since 2017, in the UK, the US and elsewhere. Perhaps now, when slave-owners are pulled down and thrown in the river, the singers of the people will come to replace them.

In the summer of 1913 Joe Hill left San Pedro and headed for Chicago. He stopped in Salt Lake City, Utah, perhaps to visit a relative there. Intending to make enough money to pay his train fare to Chicago, Hill started to work at a mine in Park City, thirty miles from Salt Lake. There he met Otto Applequist, a friend whom he had probably known earlier, in San Pedro. When Joe Hill then became ill he spent two weeks in hospital, and lost his job. He and Otto, both now unemployed, came to know some Swedish families in Sandy, Utah.

It was Christmas 1913, and the arrival of a fellow Swede who could play and sing all the old songs from back home was a real boon for the Utah Swedes. Hill became very popular, and soon he and Otto were living at the home of the Eselius family in Murray, Utah. They had of course last seen Edward and John Eselius in the hobo jungle near San Pedro. Also living at the Eselius house at Murray was a pretty, unmarried Swedish girl called Hilda Erickson. It seems that both Otto and Joe enjoyed Hilda's company.

It was on the evening of Saturday January the tenth, 1913 that Joe Hill left the Eselius house in Murray. What happened between then and around eleven thirty the same night, when he turned up at the home of Dr Frank McHugh with a bullet-hole in his chest, is a matter of debate.

Under Arrest

After Dr Frank McHugh had examined and bandaged up the recently-shot Joe Hill, the physician asked his friend Dr A.A. Bird, who was also present at the house on Fourteenth South and State Streets in Salt Lake City, to give the patient a lift back to the Eselius house. In those days, many cars still needed to be cranked to get them started or re-started, and when Bird's engine stalled *en route* the doctor got out to crank. If he hadn't had a hole right through his chest, Hill might have volunteered to do the honours.

While Bird was a-cranking, Joe Hill threw away the gun that both Bird and McHugh had seen in his possession. When they got near the Eselius house, Hill asked the doctor to turn off his headlights. Bird's passenger then proceeded to give two shrill whistles before he went in. Bird made sure that he saw Hill safely in bed before he left. At the time, Hill's friend Otto Applequist was in bed but not asleep, also at the Eselius house. After Dr Bird had left, Applequist spoke briefly with Joe Hill in his room and then left the house altogether. He was never seen or heard of again.

Dr McHugh visited Hill at the Eselius house on Monday the twelfth and Tuesday the thirteenth of January to change his patient's dressings and see how his wounds were doing. On the Tuesday, he administered a dose of morphine. On Tuesday evening, police chief Fred Peters and two deputies turned up to arrest the injured man. It seems that McHugh knew that the arrest was to take place, and had offered to drug Hill so that he would be too dopey to resist. As it happened, Peters was so jumpy about the possibility that Hill might have a gun on him that he shot his suspect as he reached for a handkerchief, hitting him in the hand.

Hill was arrested because of another local shooting that had occurred on the night when he himself had been shot. This had happened at the grocery store of John G. Morrison on West Temple and Eighth South streets in Salt Lake City.

A photo of the inside of the store published in the Salt Lake City papers in 1914 shows a narrow space with counters running down the long sides, lit by a row of gas-lights suspended from the ceiling. It was a food-shop of the old-fashioned variety, where customers were not able to pick out their own purchases, as in a modern supermarket, but were expected to ask for what they wanted while standing at a counter.

Morrison's would also appear very old-fashioned to a twenty-first century shopper because of the hundreds of cans of food on display. This was the very early days of home refrigeration: blocks of ice were still being delivered to homes and other premises, to be inserted into ice-boxes; and home freezers would not be introduced for another decade.

Shortly before ten on the night of January the tenth, John Morrison and two of his sons, Merlin and Arling, were closing up the shop when two men armed with pistols entered, wearing soft felt hats, and red bandanas over their faces, like bank-robbers in a Wild West film. One of them shouted 'We have got you now!' and they proceeded to gun down John and Arling. Merlin was at the back, heading for the store-room, and he was unscathed, but he was a horrified witness to the whole thing.

John Morrison died later, and Arling died in the store, holding his father's revolver, but it is unclear whether he managed to fire a shot. In those days it was more difficult to tell if a gun had recently been fired. An empty cartridge was found in the gun, but a witness at the subsequent trial suggested that John Morrison might have been in the habit of leaving a spent cartridge, or even an empty chamber, in his revolver at all times. Certainly none of the bullet-holes or bullets found around the store after the double murder indicated that Arling had fired, but blood was found in the street outside, and so the police assumed that at least one of the masked gunmen had been injured.

Since Joe Hill had turned up at Dr McHugh's house about ninety minutes after the shootings at Morrison's, with a fresh gunshot wound, it would have been odd if the police hadn't questioned him, once they came to know about him and his injury. Whether they should have arrested Hill, and whether he should later have been found guilty of murder, are quite different questions.

Hill was lucky, from the *medical* point of view, that the bullet-wound he sustained on January the tenth was a 'through-and-through' with the bullet exiting from his back, so that it didn't need to be dug out. If we believe that Hill was innocent of the raid on Morrison's store then the nature of the wound was unlucky from the *legal* point of view, because if the bullet had remained in him, it could have been saved after it had been retrieved. A firearms expert could then have ascertained that the bullet could not have come from John Morrison's revolver. At his trial, Hill's defence team reminded the court that if Hill had been shot 'through-and-through' at the store then the bullet would have remained on the premises, but it seems that this didn't cut any ice with the judge or the jury.

Something else that might have led to Hill's acquittal, or have prevented his going to trial in the first place (again if he was innocent of murder) would have been a detailed and circumstantial account from his own lips of where he had really been shot and by whom. If nothing else, it would have provided a partial alibi, since surely nobody would believe that, even on a Saturday night in Salt Lake City, a man could have been shot and then gone on to shoot someone somewhere else, or that anyone could have failed to be shot during a shoot-out in a store, then been shot by someone else during an unconnected incident.

If Hill was innocent and had told anyone how he had actually been shot, then the police could have questioned the real shooter and established that Hill had not been shot by Alvin Morrison, but by another man, who may then have faced a charge of attempted murder. As it was, Hill remained tight-lipped about how he had been shot that night. This was in keeping with his usual habit of not giving away much about himself.

Another 'if' concerns the pistol Hill had thrown out of Dr Bird's car on the way back to the Eseliuses, which was never found. If he had kept it and the police had accepted that it was his gun, or a gun that was in his possession that night, then they may have been able to determine that it could not have been the weapon that had killed either Alvin or John Morrison. There is even a possibility that it was the very gun that had been used to shoot Hill, and that he had snatched it from the man who had shot him, whoever that was.

In Joe Hill, the Salt Lake City police had a murder suspect who had been shot on the night that a murderer had, they thought, been shot. Hill had not, however, been the only man who had been shot in the city on that Saturday night, and survived. Nineteen year-old Oran Anderson had been shot in the arm, and walked not to a doctor but to a police station, to report it. He maintained that he had been held up and shot by two men in the street. The police believed him, and he was quickly dismissed as a suspect in the Morrison case.

Two police officers went to great lengths to capture two more suspects, C.E. Christensen and Joe Woods. They were trying to get out of Salt Lake City by hopping onto a freight train, but the cops persuaded them to hop off by subjecting them to a hail of bullets. They were later locked up for an earlier robbery in Arizona, but, like Oran Anderson, they were not arrested for the Morrison attack.

A man known as W.J. Williams was arrested near the Morrison store and found to have a bloody handkerchief in his pocket, but he also was quickly released. An ex-convict called Frank Wilson was also seen boarding a streetcar on the night of the murders: he was hunched over and seemed distracted, and may have been concealing a gun-shot wound. He was raw-boned like Hill, and for a while after Hill's arrest the police thought Hill and Wilson were one and the same. But once they had established who Joe was, they lost interest in Frank.

It seems that the police started dismissing other suspects far too soon after they arrested Joe Hill. Evidently, they were persuaded not just by the fact that he had been shot on the same night Alvin and John Morrison had been killed, and would not explain how. Hill was also known to have possessed a gun, which he had thrown away. He also had a friend, Otto Applequist, who had disappeared before Hill's arrest. This looked suspicious: was Applequist the second gunman in the Morrison shooting?

Fans of TV detective series will know that a criminal usually has means, motive and opportunity to carry out a crime. Hill certainly had means – a gun – and opportunity – he was out and about in Salt Lake City on the night of the murders. But what was his motive? Not robbery, surely, as nothing had been taken from Morrison's store. Nobody could prove that Hill had any reason to kill John Morrison, although some assumed that something may have happened between them that had turned the blood bad during Hill's time in Salt Lake City.

The fact that one of the gunmen had shouted 'We have got you now' before the shooting started suggests that the attackers had been out to get John Morrison at least, and even that they might have tried and failed to kill him before. This was entirely in line with the fact that Morrison had previously survived two attacks by gunmen, and that he had confided in friends that he believed that persons he never named were indeed out to get him. These were supposed to be bitter enemies he had made in his previous career as a Salt Lake City police officer. It was even suggested that since one of these attacks had happened in 1913, Joe Hill might have been involved on that occasion.

The revenge theory explains the gunmen's failure to rob Morrison's store, the phrase they had shouted and the fact that they did not shoot Merlin, the younger son. They probably only meant to kill John, and killed Alvin in self-defence when he drew his father's gun. If anyone could have established that Hill had had any contact with Morrison, let alone opportunity to build up a deadly grudge against him, then Hill could have been shown to have had means, opportunity and motive. But no motive was discovered.

On Trial

At Hill's arraignment – a pre-trial hearing – Joe represented himself because he could not afford a lawyer. This hardly mattered, since in the US the main purpose of such hearings is to establish if the case has sufficient 'legs', in terms of evidence in particular, to be worth the time, effort and expense of a proper trial.

Although it was later argued that Hill's case should never have got past the arraignment stage, it would have been very surprising if the matter had actually been abandoned at this point. At his trial proper, Hill was represented by two lawyers who volunteered to help him *pro bono*. Their names were E.D. McDougall and F.B. Scott, and although in theory Joe should have been very grateful and cooperative in his relations with them, they must have found him a very difficult client.

On June the nineteenth 1914, the third day of the trial, Hill began to suspect that Scott and McDougall were working against him, and doing him more harm than good. He stood up while the session was in full flow, and declared, 'I have three prosecuting attorneys here, and I intend to get rid of two of them.' He then proceeded to fire his defence lawyers, and announced, 'I will act as my own attorney after this, and cross-examine all the witnesses, and I think I will make a good job of it.'

At this point, Scott and McDougall might have walked out, as Hill had told them to do, but judge Morris L. Ritchie insisted that they stay behind and carry on. Ritchie did, however, allow Joe to cross-examine witnesses after his counsel had finished with them. Eventually the judge decided to let Hill's defence lawyers remain as *amici curiae*, or friends of the court. This was a status usually given to independent advisors who, for instance, had persuaded a judge that they had useful information for the court, although they had not been called as witnesses. That Ritchie asked Scott and McDougall to stay on those terms, when Hill had a perfect right to dismiss them, is just one of the unusual and controversial aspects of the trial of Joe Hill.

After the lunch-time recess, Hill, who had ended the morning with no lawyers to defend him, returned to the court-room with three. Both nationally and locally, the IWW had organised a response to Joe Hill's plight, and on the afternoon of the third day of the trial half of that response appeared, in the form of Soren X. Christensen, a prominent local attorney engaged by the Wobblies.

One can't help feeling sorry for Christensen. He was joining the defence team in a murder case on the afternoon of the third day, and had just walked in on a hot-headed dispute between the defendant and his existing counsel (which seems, however, to have been resolved before the afternoon session commenced). Christensen probably knew that Hill had originally refused to accept any Wobbly involvement in his case, and he certainly knew that to some extent he,

Christensen, would only be marking time in Salt Lake City until the big gun arrived. The big gun was Orrin N. Hilton, a very distinguished lawyer and a judge in his own right, who had also been engaged by the Wobblies, but whose participation in Hill's case would be delayed by commitments in Michigan.

To add to Christensen's woes, the afternoon of the nineteenth of June kicked off with the appearance of Phoebe Seeley, the prosecution's best witness. She was one of a number of people who had seen and heard something connected with the raid on Morrison's store on the fateful night itself. The number of witnesses may have been connected to the fact that the gunmen, whoever they were, had picked Saturday night to attack Morrison. This would have made some sense if they had been planning to make off with the day's takings, which may have been higher than usual on a Saturday; but as we know, they didn't take anything.

Mrs Seeley and her husband Frank had walked past John Morrison's store on their way home from the theatre, just before the attack on the evening of the tenth of January. As they got further away from the store, they were forced off the pavement by two men walking abreast. The men were assumed to have been the gunmen, but they cannot have been wearing their bandanas quite yet, as Phoebe was able to get a detailed look at the taller of the two men. Her description tallied closely with Joe Hill's appearance, but Mrs Seeley never claimed to be one hundred percent certain that she had seen Hill that night in the street. She had, however, seen a tall, thin man with light hair, a sharp nose and scars on his face and neck.

When, on June the twenty-seventh, the jury retired to consider their verdict, what they had seen and heard in court on the nineteenth may have had more of an influence over their deliberations than some of the other days of the trial. It was then that they had seen the accused frankly admitting that he thought the trial was going badly for him, accusing his lawyers of treachery, then re-appearing with an additional lawyer engaged by the IWW. Despite the Wobblies who had been attending the trial, this was, according to Gibbs Smith's 1969 book on Hill, the moment at which everybody realised that Hill was a Wobbly himself. Mrs Seeley's testimony, given on the same day, must also have made a big impression on the jury.

It is likely that at least some members of Joe Hill's jury thought a lot less of him after they had learned that he was an IWW activist. In 1912, the year before Hill had arrived in Utah, there had been a big strike at the copper mine at Bingham Canyon outside Salt Lake City. The miners, many of whom were Greek immigrants, were not just mad at the mine-owners. They also resented one Leonidas Skliris, a Greek like themselves, who had a baleful influence over their lives although he did not work directly for the company.

Known as 'the Czar of the Greeks', Skliris was, among other things, one of those crooked employment agents, who demanded that workers make him an up-front payment, and even regular payments thereafter, to obtain and stay in a job. This was called the 'padrone' system, which the company denied even existed. Much of the money the miners retained after they had paid Skliris had to be spent in shops that were part of the man's grubby little empire. Skliris was also more than willing to supply workers to break strikes: he had done this at Murray, Utah, where Hill would later lodge with the Eseliuses, in 1912.

The strikers at Bingham, nearly five thousand of them, demanded union recognition, a pay-rise of fifty cents a day, and the removal of Leonidas Skliris. Realising that the mine owners would probably try to send in strike-breaking workers to replace them (likely supplied by Skliris) some of the strikers armed themselves with rifles and took up positions on a nearby mountain, ready to repel any newcomers. This was a very risky strategy, but then the miners were taking huge risks every day they worked at Bingham. In 1911 alone, four hundred men had died while working there.

William Spry, the governor of Utah who was later deeply involved in Joe Hill's case, attempted to disperse the armed pickets by leading seventy-five deputies up the mountain to confront them. But the strikers stood firm, and Spry was forced to retreat. In an unfounded burst of confidence, Leonidas Skliris offered five thousand dollars to anyone who could prove that he had been extorting money from the workers. When one of the strikers came forward to claim the money, Skliris, like Spry, had to back down.

Like many strikes, the one at Bingham gradually dissolved, despite the initial resolve of the strikers. The strikers had, however, won recognition for their union, and got rid of Skliris. They also got half the pay-rise they had asked for – twenty-five cents a day rather than fifty. Mining has continued at the Bingham Canyon mine since 1912: in fact the mine itself was opened in 1906: its rich mineral deposits had been discovered by two Mormon brothers, Sanford and Thomas Bingham, in 1848. The Bingham excavations are now considered the biggest hole ever dug by human beings in the surface of the earth, and the deepest open-cast mine in the world. It has also produced more copper than any other copper-mine in history. Its historical importance was recognised in 1966 when it was designated a National Historic Landmark.

It is hard to prove any great participation in the Bingham strike by the IWW, and it seems to be practically certain that Joe Hill was not there. The union on the ground, which initially had very few members among the miners, was the Western Federation of Miners or WFM. It may, however, have been immaterial to the Utah authorities and members of Joe Hill's jury, whether any Wobblies had been at Bingham. They may have regarded all strikers and union agitators as dangerous troublemakers, whatever their loyalties or political beliefs.

Whether their thoughts were swayed by memories of the Bingham strike and other labour disputes, it was now the duty of Joe Hill's jury to decide if the evidence presented to them justified a guilty or a not-guilty verdict. In the many pro-Joe letters, speeches, telegrams and articles that followed the verdict and sentencing, the fact that all this evidence was circumstantial was repeatedly mentioned. It is not the case, however, that circumstantial evidence is always unreliable, or that suspects should never be found guilty on circumstantial evidence alone. If circumstantial evidence in a particular case is consistent and convincing, and cannot easily be contradicted, it can lead to a perfectly correct conviction.

Imagine if you spent most of last Friday away from home, and returned late at night to find your laptop missing from your kitchen. There is no sign of a break-in, and you are certain that the only person apart from yourself who has a key to your place is your ex-girlfriend Sophie (you intended to get the key back from her, or change the locks, but you have never got round to it).

You have reliable information from mutual friends that Sophie's own laptop recently stopped working when her new girlfriend spilled soup on it. You also know that she is out of work, low on cash and in need of a laptop to surf the internet for a new job. To cap it all, on Saturday morning one of your neighbours tells you that on Friday he saw a woman answering Sophie's description leaving your house carrying a large rucksack that could easily have concealed a laptop.

So far all of your evidence that Sophie might have stolen your laptop is circumstantial, but there is certainly enough here to justify your contacting Sophie about the missing laptop, or even asking the local police to look into it. The police might even decide that there is enough evidence to justify their searching Sophie's place. Hard evidence (as opposed to circumstantial evidence) might then appear, in the form of your laptop sitting on Sophie's sofa.

Circumstantial as it is, your initial evidence of Sophie's guilt is much stronger than the similarly circumstantial evidence that put Joe Hill in front of a firing-squad. After all, Sophie had means, motive and opportunity. She had means, in the form of the key to your house; and motive: she needed a laptop. Her opportunity presented itself when she somehow found out that you would be away from home on Friday.

There is also nothing to weaken any of the links in your chain of circumstantial evidence regarding Sophie's crime. Sophie didn't come into a shedload of money two days before her raid on your house. Nobody saw a strange man picking the lock on your front door on Friday afternoon. Sophie's brother didn't lend her a laptop on Thursday, and she didn't get a job offer on Friday morning.

No convincing motive was ever found for Joe Hill's supposed attack on the Morrisons, and several links in the chain of circumstantial evidence were decidedly weak. It was far from certain that Alvin Morrison actually managed to fire a shot at the gunmen, and if he had, the bullet was not found in the store, as it should have been if it had gone right through Joe Hill. Mrs Seeley always insisted that she was not entirely sure she had seen Hill that night, and nobody else got as clear a look at either of the attackers as she did.

Though there was blood in the street outside, the technology of the time could only determine that it was mammalian blood: it could have been the blood of an injured dog. And a Dr Beer had testified at the trial that the bullet-hole in Hill's jacket, which was four inches below the hole in his chest, only made sense if Hill had been holding his hands above his head when he was shot. Merlin Morrison, John's son who had witnessed the whole thing, had not seen either of the gunmen raise their hands in this way.

Hill's attorneys tried to convince the court that their client should be acquitted because the state's chain of circumstantial evidence against him had these and other weak links and contradictions. But Judge Ritchie rejected this idea, implying while delivering his instructions to the jury that circumstantial evidence didn't need to form a perfect chain – it need only be like a cable, that might still work if several strands of it were frayed or broken. In this respect, Ritchie's instructions went right against the Utah legal code that applied at the time, which stated that 'where the state seeks to convict a defendant upon circumstantial evidence . . . [the] chain of evidence must be complete and unbroken and established beyond reasonable doubt'.

Judge Ritchie had made a serious mistake in his instructions to the jury about the use of circumstantial evidence. Earlier, Hill's attorney Ernest McDougall had made an even more grievous mistake during his contribution to the summing-up for the defence. Riding roughshod over courtroom etiquette, McDougall attacked Mrs Seeley, asserting that 'I believe her testimony was a frame up'. He then stated that the whole judicial system in Utah was corrupt, that the Utahns did not accept that a defendant was innocent until proven guilty, and that Elmer Leatherwood, the prosecuting attorney in Hill's case, was merely trying to make a name for himself, to 'make a record before the people' to further his political ambitions.

McDougall might have done better to have complimented the Utahns on their beautiful state and its charming state capital, remarked on their sense of fair play, and ended with something like the sentence, 'I cannot believe that the enlightened air of this fine place can ever be tainted with the poison of prejudice or ignorance'.

Instead, McDougall scored a horrendous own goal, and the wily Leatherwood was more than ready to take full advantage of his opponent's mistake. He pretended to take McDougall's criticism of Mrs Seeley as a snipe at the women of Utah in general, and asserted that they 'are shoulder to shoulder with men in the great accomplishments in every line of life'. Leatherwood also feigned righteous indignation, asserting that:

When a man charges . . . that juries are corrupt, and public officers are false to their trust and intimates that Utah's a state where a man cannot procure a fair trial, when he strikes at the very root of our American institutions of justice and freedom, I resent it.

In his summation, Leatherwood also painted a lurid picture of how conditions in Utah might degenerate if the men of the jury did not find Hill guilty:

Gentlemen, it is for such as you to say how long this sort of thing shall go on. It is for you in the performance of the high duty you are called upon to perform to put a stop to the making of widows and orphans in this manner by enforcing the penalty of the law on such men as go about shooting down peaceable and law abiding citizens.

Leatherwood also hinted to the jury that Hill was a member of an organisation that, in his view, was full of 'those parasites on society who murder and rob rather than make an honest living'.

The men of the jury (it was unusual for women to sit on juries in Utah at this time) returned a guilty verdict. After sentencing Hill to death, Judge Ritchie asked him if he would prefer to shot or hanged. With typical bravado, Joe replied, 'I'll take shooting. I'm used to that. I have been shot a few times in the past and I guess I can stand it again'.

Outrage

Although the majority of the press and the public in Utah seem to have been happy with the verdict and sentence, there was a great deal of unhappiness elsewhere, and many groups and individuals started to strain every muscle to get Joe Hill acquitted, re-tried or pardoned, or at least to have his sentence commuted to life in prison. Among others who got caught up in the campaign to save Joe were the local Swedish consul, the Swedish ambassador to the US, many members of the IWW, Woodrow Wilson (the president who would take America into the Great War in April 1917) and Helen Keller.

Keller (1880-1968) was the remarkable deaf-blind woman who managed to communicate via her partially-sighted, hearing teacher and companion. A native of Alabama, Keller studied at Harvard and was the first deaf-blind person to be awarded a university degree. She became an important writer, lecturer and advocate for people with disabilities and sensory impairments. She was also a Wobbly, having joined the IWW in 1912. In an interview published in the *New York Tribune* in January 1916, she revealed that she had turned from religion to socialism after finding out more about the conditions in which hard-up people lived and worked. In particular, she learned that some types of blindness could be caused by bad working conditions, and by syphilis caught by poor women driven to prostitution. IWW boss Bill Haywood could have told her about blindness caused by accidents: he had been blinded in one eye, and as a consequence is usually seen in profile, or turned to his right, in photographs.

Keller was also nudged to the left by reading Marx (who had written articles for the *New York Tribune*), hearing about the Lawrence, Massachusetts textile-workers strike (of which more later) and reading H.G. Wells' 1908 book *New Worlds for Old*, an explanation of socialism. 'It seemed as if I had been asleep and waked to a new world', Keller told the *Tribune* reporter, Barbara Bindley. When Keller told her interviewer that she had become an 'industrialist', Bindley was 'surprised out of composure'. 'You don't mean an IWW - a syndicalist?' she asked.

Most Wobblies were opposed to the war then raging in Europe – surely it was a case of workers fighting against workers, when they should have been uniting to fight against the capitalist imperialists who had put them in the trenches in the first place? In contrast, Keller's attitude was that the Great War was a training-ground for the future revolution: 'don't forget workers are getting their discipline in the trenches . . . they are acquiring the will to combat'. How she imagined this would work in the case of a German soldier decapitated by a British spade during hand-to-hand combat is anyone's guess. Unfortunately, Joe Hill had the same attitude. In a September 1915 letter written from prison to his friend Sam Murray, he suggested that:

All these silly priests and old maid sewing circles that are moaning about peace at this time should be locked up in the crazy house as a menace to society. The war is the finest training school for rebels in the world and for anti-militarists as well . . .

It may be that Hill and Keller's idea of the war as a training-ground for revolutionaries was a case of trying to see a silver lining even in the darkest possible cloud. Hill's experience as an armed revolutionary in Mexico may have fed into his thinking on the war in Europe: perhaps he felt that if they'd all received training in a regular army, the Magonistas may have done better against the *Federales*?

Helen Keller wrote direct to Woodrow Wilson about the Hill case: the president received her telegram just three days before Joe's execution. Addressing Wilson as 'the official father of all the people', Keller asserted that 'Joseph Hillstrom has not had a fair trial and the sentence passed upon him is unjust'. She pleaded for the president to intervene to delay the execution and demand a new trial. This would 'give the man justice to which the laws of the land entitle him'.

Wilson's answer to Keller was sent off the next morning. He professed himself 'very much touched' by her message, but asserted that 'the matter lies entirely beyond my jurisdiction and power'. That afternoon he did, however, send a telegram to the governor of Utah urging 'the justice and advisability, if it be possible, of a thorough reconsideration of the case of Joseph Hillstrom'.

Governor William Spry stuck to his guns, however, and his reply to the president asserted that there was no reason for Wilson's intervention, as 'a fair and impartial trial' in Utah had established 'the guilt of one of the perpetrators of one of the most atrocious murders ever committed in this state'.

Spry also mentioned the 'thousands of threatening letters demanding the release of Hillstrom regardless of his guilt or innocence'. The governor may have associated these 'threatening letters' with claims by IWW members and others that they would liberate Joe by force. At a huge protest meeting held in Manhattan on November the eighth, a speaker called James Larkin demanded that 'the case of Joseph Hillstrom go to the greatest jury of all – the jury of the workers. Let the working class pass judgment and liberate Joe Hill. If we but say the word nothing can stop us'.

Writing in the IWW magazine *Solidarity* on the thirteenth of November, John Sandgren all but claimed that a revolution was in order: 'only by shaking the country to the foundations,' Sandgren wrote, 'will we prevail over the evil powers that control the fate of our beloved fellow worker, Joe Hill'. The possibility of civil disorder, for instance in the form of a raid on Hill's prison, only encouraged the Utah officials to strengthen security around themselves, their meetings and the prison itself.

Then as now, some IWW members and supporters believed, as Hill's clumsy defence-lawyer Ernest McDougall had implied in court, that Joe Hill was tried and found guilty because he had been deliberately framed by the Utah authorities, who used the coincidence of his having received a gunshot wound on that fateful Saturday night in Salt Lake to rid the world of what they saw as an enemy of the *status quo*. Gibbs Smith and others doubted that this is what actually happened, but Wobblies had certainly been framed in this way before.

In December 1905 Frank Steunenberg, a former governor of Idaho who had clashed with the unions, was killed by a bomb planted near his house in Caldwell, Idaho. The perpetrator, a slimy character called Harry Orchard, was quickly arrested, then persuaded to implicate IWW boss Bill Haywood and three of his comrades in the crime. They were supposed to have conspired with Orchard, though none of them were in Idaho at the time.

Luckily, Haywood and the other accused were defended by, among others, the celebrated courtroom performer Clarence Darrow, who helped to make mincemeat of the prosecution case. The attempt to frame Haywood and the others backfired on the authorities: when he was acquitted, 'Big Bill' became an instant folk hero.

Later, in 1917, Haywood was one of one hundred and sixty-five Wobblies arrested under a new law Woodrow Wilson's government had brought in, supposedly to help the war effort. Accused of hindering America's attempts to support the Allies in the Great War, Haywood was sentenced to twenty years. As we know, Ricardo Flores Magón, the inspiration for the white Magonistas, including Joe Hill, had been arrested, tried and found guilty under the same 1917 Espionage Act, and had also been sentenced to twenty years. In 1921 Bill Haywood skipped bail and defected to communist Russia, where he died in 1928. As in the case of Flores Magón, diabetes played a role in the early death of Haywood, but in Bill's case his alcoholism made matters worse.

Another victim of new laws brought in under wartime conditions was the great Black Wobbly Ben Fletcher, who had helped organise the dockers of Philadelphia. Fletcher was sentenced to ten years in the Leavenworth federal prison in

Kansas, where the Mexican revolutionary Ricardo Flores Magón would die in 1922.

The official attempt to implicate Bill Haywood and others in the fatal bombing of Frank Steunenberg certainly looks like an attempt to 'frame' individuals whom the authorities found to be troublesome. Another clear case of 'framing' was associated with the Lawrence, Massachusetts textile workers strike of 1912.

The Lawrence strike was one of the most impressive that the IWW helped to organise. The workers; men, women and children from a range of different nationalities, began the strike over a reduction in pay, but as the dispute progressed the atrocious conditions under which many had been working were gradually revealed. On average, the workers were earning less than nine dollars a week, and some had to pay more than half of this to rent tiny flats in overcrowded tenement buildings that were also fire-traps. Children as young as fourteen were working long hours at the looms, and many of them died just a few years after starting work. Most workers could only afford to eat bread, molasses and beans.

The IWW sent twenty-seven year-old Joseph Ettor to Lawrence to help organise the strike. Ettor was perfectly suited to the job: he could speak English, Italian and Polish, and could also understand Hungarian and Yiddish. Under his leadership, the strikers demanded a fifteen percent increase in wages and double-time for overtime. Mass pickets and street demonstrations featuring marching and singing were organised. A few days into the strike, a Wobbly called Arturo Giovanitti, who was a poet among other things, arrived to organise strike relief. This included soup kitchens, free medical care from volunteer doctors, and strike pay.

Just over a week into the strike, a picketer called Anna LoPizzo was shot dead, probably by a local police officer. The police arrested a striker called Joseph Caruso, supposedly for the murder, and also arrested Ettor and Giovanitti as accessories, although the latter two were three miles away at the time of the shooting, talking to a group of German workers. Their trial didn't happen until September, although there were extensive IWW strikes and demonstrations demanding the release of the three men.

In the same way that the Swedes rallied around Joe Hill, the Italians in America and back home showed their support for what we might call the Lawrence Three. Although they all had cast-iron alibis, and Caruso wasn't even a member of the IWW, Ettor, Giovanitti and Caruso had to endure three months locked in cages in the court-room at Salem, listening to legal arguments, before they were acquitted.

As we know, Helen Keller's route to the political left was partly influenced by stories of the Lawrence strike. She also wrote an introduction to *Arrows in the Gale*, a 1914 book of English translations of Arturo Giovanitti's poems. 'As a poet,' she wrote, 'he is to be judged by his success in rendering these ideas in verse, and not by his relations to Syndicalism or Socialism or any other movement in which he happens to be active. The laws of poetic beauty and power, not one's beliefs about the economic world, determine the excellence of his work.'

The authorities in Utah in 1914 certainly had more reason to think of Joe Hill as a likely murder suspect than the law in Massachusetts had had to see Ettor, Giovanitti and Caruso in the same light back in 1912. One reason why Hill was not acquitted as the three Italians had been was his refusal to provide an alibi.

Governor Spry had closed his angry telegram to Woodrow Wilson by asserting that 'tangible facts must be presented before I will further interfere in this case'. The 'tangible facts' that would have saved Hill would surely have included details of how he had really received his gunshot wound on that fateful night in January 1914, which might have added up to an alibi. But Hill held fast to his resolution not to reveal how this had happened, even though he had been offered a deal whereby, if he had told the full story, he might have been pardoned and the details of the real shooting revealed only to the prison warden, his lawyers and some investigators.

Since relatively little is known about any part of Joe Hill's life, would-be biographers have tended to pick through the letters Hill sent from prison in Salt Lake City, hoping to find clues. They certainly do yield some information, for instance in favour of the theory that Hill really did fight alongside the Magonistas south of the border, but the overall impression the reader gets from them is of the writer's fondness for his friends and his robust cheerfulness, astonishing in a man writing from Death Row. True, Hill sometimes wrote these letters when Judge Hilton and others were assuring him that he would be acquitted, but the generally positive tone still seems amazing, given the context.

In the letters, his primary concern seems to be to reach out to his friends and fellow-workers, to encourage them and help them banish any bad feelings they may have about their incarcerated friend's dire situation. The correspondence also shows that the prisoner felt supported by his friends on the outside, and believed that they were doing everything they could for him.

Prison letters written to Joe's friend Sam Murray in California were published in the monthly *Industrial Pioneer* magazine in 1923. In a letter dated September the fifteenth 1914 Hill insists that he is 'feeling well under the circumstances and I am fortunate enough to have the ability to entertain myself and to look at everything from the bright side'. A later letter reveals that one way Hill could 'entertain' himself was with music: 'have been busy working on some musical composition and whenever I get an "inspiration" I can't quit until it's finished'.

Later in the September letter to Murray, Hill assures Sam that 'there is nothing you could do for me. I know you would if you could'. This and other letters, to Sam and other correspondents, including Elizabeth Gurley Flynn, are signed off with phrases such as 'Yours for the OBU', meaning the One Big Union.

Even when Hill was writing to Murray for the last time, when he thought he was to be shot in the next twenty-four hours, Joe was joking that 'this dying business is not quite so bad as it is cracked up to be' and concluding, cheerily:

Well, Sam, you and me had a little pleasure at one time that few rebels have had the privilege of having, and I guess I've had my share of the fun after all. Now, just forget me, and say goodbye to the bunch.

Yours for the OBU,

JOE HILL

The details of Joe Hill's execution, early in the morning on the nineteenth of November 1915, still have the power to both horrify and enrage. He woke at about five and started to tear up his blankets. He used the strips to tie around the bars of his cell so that the door could not be opened. Then he put his mattress against the door. When his guards tried to cut through all this, he jabbed at them with a broom-handle that he had broken in two to give him a jagged edge. All this would have been impossible in the last days of judicial executions in the UK, when an entire wall of the condemned cell would open, revealing the hangman and his noose waiting beyond.

When Hill was eventually persuaded to come quietly he was led out into the prison yard and strapped to a chair twenty feet away from the jail's blacksmith's shop. The five men of the firing squad were hidden inside the shop, behind a canvas curtain cut with holes for their rifles. Four guns had live bullets: the last was loaded with a blank. Joe was blindfolded, and a doctor came with a stethoscope and pinned a paper target over his heart. This macabre detail is remembered in Si Kahn's 1976 song *Paper Heart*:

> There's a man shot dead in Utah
> With a paper heart pinned on him
> Framed up without pardon
> I guess you know his name.

Before the order to fire was given, Joe smiled and shouted 'Fire – go on and fire!'

Hill's attempt to seal up his cell early that morning seems particularly extraordinary in view of the fact that he could have walked free if only he had told the authorities in Utah who had actually shot him on that fateful night in 1914. The alibi that might have saved poor Joe, and which he refused to give, was revealed by William Adler in his 2011 book on Hill, *The Man Who Never Died*.

Adler discovered that in the 1940s a writer called Aubrey Haan was researching a novel and contacted Hilda Erickson, the pretty, unmarried Swedish girl whom both Joe Hill and Otto Applequist had come to know while living with the Eseliuses near Salt Lake City. In a letter, Hilda revealed to Haan that she had been engaged to Otto Applequist, but that she had broken it off. The spurned lover assumed that she 'liked Joe better than him' and later 'shot him in a fit of anger', though he 'was sorry right after'. Hilda's letter even reveals that Otto had somehow 'carried' Joe to Doctor McHugh's office, and that Hill had perhaps provoked the attack by teasing Otto about Hilda, saying 'that he was going to take me away from him'.

If we put this revelation together with the partial account Hill gave to Doctors McHugh and Bird on the night in question, we can begin to construct a fuller picture of what might have happened. Hill claimed that he had 'got into a stew with a friend of mine who thought I had insulted his wife'. According to Hilda, the 'stew' had been over herself, not the friend's wife but his ex-fiancée, but Joe may have been confused by pain and shock, or may have substituted the word 'wife' to throw those present in McHugh's office off the scent, much as a newspaper or magazine might change the names of some of the people in a sensitive story in order to anonymise those involved.

According to what he said that night, Hill responded to the suggestion that he had insulted the man's wife by knocking him down. The man, whom we must now assume was Otto Applequist, then pulled a gun on Joe. To judge from the bullet-hole in Joe's knitted jacket, four inches below the hole in his chest, Hill raised his hands high above his head when he saw the gun. He might have done better to have just run away. The shooter 'didn't really know what he was doing', which suggests that he was either drunk or mad with rage, or both. Since Joe turned up at the doctor's house with a gun, we might assume that he somehow took it from Otto, who might have dropped it as soon as he had fired it, horrified at what he had just done, or tried to do.

We know that Joe Hill later threw the gun away, and that when he returned to the Eselius house he had a quick word with Otto, who then vanished into the night. According to Hilda Erickson's letter to Aubrey Haan, Hill told her that he had been shot by Otto, but advised her not to say anything about it to anyone. Evidently, he kept quiet, and insisted on Hilda's silence, to protect Otto from a possible charge of attempted murder. He may also have thought that it might damage Hilda's prospects in life if it became known that two hoboes, one of them with a gun, had been fighting over her. Hilda Erickson visited Joe every Sunday in prison, until his execution. They spoke both English and Swedish together.

It seems that the secret did not stay between Joe and Hilda. Another Utah Swede, Olaf Lindegren, wrote to Governor Spry in September 1915, telling him the whole story. In his letter, Lindegren suggested that Hill may have wanted to keep the truth about his shooting secret because he did not want to drag the Eseliuses into the case: 'as Hillstrom and this family were strong friends, fraternity brothers and countrymen, it is only natural to suppose that Hillstrom will not bring them into the case at any price'.

Lindegren's letter, written in rather broken English, mentions Otto Applequist, but is vague about how or why the shooting might have taken place. Olaf advises that Spry should only 'enquire of the girl Hilda' with 'great precaution' and he begs the governor to keep his, Olaf's, letter secret. Spry seems to have gone one better (or worse) and completely ignored it. If he had sent police officers to question Hilda and the Eseliuses the alibi Hill refused to supply might have slotted into place, and Joe might have been set free.

If the authorities had freed Joe Hill after following up Olaf Lindegren's letter, they may then have had to re-open the Morrison murder case and look for an alternative suspect. Adler fancies a man called Magnus Olson as the actual murderer. Olson, a Scandinavian like Hill, may have been the 'Frank Wilson' who was spotted acting suspiciously on a Salt Lake City streetcar on the night of the murders. 'Frank Wilson' was just one of Olson's aliases: others, like 'Magnus Osberg' sound more Scandinavian, but the Norwegian also used aliases that suggested an Irish background, such as 'Magnus Moran' and 'Tim Hurley'.

Olson was a career criminal who served jail time in around nine different US states. His crimes, which had started when he was quite young, included theft, arson and attempted murder. He had been in the Utah State Prison from 1911 to Christmas 1912, and had also been spotted in Salt Lake City by a prison officer on the night of the Morrison shootings. He had been arrested as a suspect in these murders, and the police had found a bloody handkerchief on his person, but for some reason they had quickly released him.

As we know, Olson looked so much like Hill that when the police arrested Joe, at first they thought he had given a false name and that he actually was Olson (though they knew the man in question as Wilson or perhaps Williams). This despite the fact that they had police photos of 'Wilson'. Both men were tall and slim, and had blue eyes and light-brown hair. They were roughly the same age, Olson having been born in Tromsø, Norway in 1881. The inference is that Phoebe Seeley, the state's best witness at Joe Hill's trial, had seen Olson that night and not Hill at all. The slight differences between the looks of Joe and Magnus were perhaps the reason that she never felt one hundred percent certain that she had actually seen Joe near the Morrisons' store that night.

Whether Olson killed the Morrisons or not, it cannot be said that his arrest as a suspect in the Morrison shooting, or his time in jail in Utah, made him change his ways. Just two weeks after the Morrisons were killed he was arrested again, for robbing a train in Elko, Nevada. Later he became a body-guard for the famous gangster Al Capone, and may have been involved in the St Valentine's Day Massacre that took place in 1929. On that occasion, seven men were gunned down in a Chicago warehouse. The getaway car used by the assailants, who have never been identified, belonged to Magnus Olson.

Joe Hill was determined not to be buried in Utah, and in fact he was cremated at the Graceland Cemetery in Chicago, the city where Magnus Olson would later find another niche as a dangerous criminal. In a service at Chicago's West Side Auditorium, Hill's songs were sung, Judge Hilton and Bill Haywood spoke to the people, and later, at the cemetery itself, speeches were given in Swedish, Russian, Hungarian, Polish,

Spanish, German, Italian, Yiddish and Lithuanian. The events at the hall and the cemetery were attended by thousands. In Chicago itself, the streets were completely blocked. Describing the procession from the hall to the 'el' station at Van Buren and Halsted, Ralph Chaplin wrote:

Slowly and impressively the vast throng moved through the west side streets. Windows flew open at its approach and were filled with peering faces. Porches and even roofs were blackened with people, and some of the more daring were lined up over signboards and on telephone and arc-light poles. The flower-bearers, with their bright coloured floral pieces and wreaths tied with crimson ribbons, formed a walking garden almost a block in length.

The coffin rode in a special train to the cemetery, where what Chaplin calls a 'vast audience' soon assembled in the open air. Here there were more speeches, and singing that went on till dusk. The next day, the body was cremated, and the story of what happened to the ashes is quite extraordinary.

They were split up between six hundred small envelopes and sent all over the world to be scattered to the winds. This was in keeping with Joe's last will, which he wrote out as verse on the last day of his life:

My Last Will

My will is easy to decide,
For there is nothing to divide.
My kin don't need to fuss and moan -
"Moss does not cling to a rolling stone."

My body? — Oh! — If I could choose,
I would to ashes it reduce,
And let the merry breezes blow
My dust to where some flowers grow.

Perhaps some fading flower then
Would come to life and bloom again.
This is my last and final will.
Good luck to all of you,
Joe Hill

The sequel to the widespread scattering of Joe Hill's ashes came in 1988, when the US postal service revealed that back in the day it had taken one envelope out of the mail because of its 'subversive potential'. In '88, the last envelope of Joe's ashes was handed over to the IWW, and a pinch of the ashes was swallowed by the English activist and singer Billy Bragg. Mark Levy's song *Joe Hill's Ashes*, one of at least two songs with this title, tells the tale of the last envelope:

We sing his songs to fan the flames and talk about him much.
The ashes of this rebel voice are still too hot to touch.

The phrase 'fan the flames' comes from the title of early editions of the so-called Big Red Songbook: *I.W.W. Songs to Fan the Flames of Discontent*.

The Songs

As the last mourners left Chicago's Graceland cemetery, those who had been present throughout the whole day had the comfort of knowing that they had sung through, or at least heard, the entire Joe Hill songbook, and perhaps helped to 'fan the flames of discontent'.

It is better to listen to songs – better still to sing or play them – than to read about them. Even reading the lyrics of some otherwise excellent songs, detached from the music, can be disappointing. Joe Hill seems not to have been the kind of song-writer who wrote the words first and then set them to music. There are accounts of him sitting at pianos – for instance in union halls or mission halls – trying out both words and music together.

For the most part, he took the words of popular songs of the day and changed them to suit his own purposes, recycling the tunes. His *The Preacher and the Slave*, written in 1911, is set to the music of the popular hymn *In the Sweet Bye and Bye,* a Christian anthem that was first published in 1868. The hymn, with original lyrics by S. Fillmore Bennett and music by Joseph P. Webster, is a simple, repetitive and rather sentimental statement of longing for the heaven promised to Christians who have lived a good life:

> We shall sing on that beautiful shore
> The melodious songs of the blessed;
> And our spirit shall sorrow no more,
> Not a sigh for the blessing of rest.

For religious sceptics, and even for many committed Christians, there is often a lingering suspicion that some preachers offer the promise of a reward in heaven to pacify the hungry and the oppressed, who might otherwise rise up and fight to improve their lives. Joe Hill's new words to the old *Sweet Bye and Bye* tune describe this scenario. Because the song is called *The Preacher and the Slave*, we know that at least the first verse is supposed to be about the missionaries who used to preach to slaves:

> Long-haired preachers come out every night,
> Try to tell you what's wrong and what's right;
> But when asked how 'bout something to eat
> They will answer with voices so sweet

The answer comes in the chorus, which describes heaven as a kind of all-you-can-eat buffet:

> You will eat, bye and bye,
> In that glorious land above the sky;
> Work and pray, live on hay,

You'll get pie in the sky when you die.

The idea of a heaven where food is plentiful is reminiscent of 'Haywire Mac' McClintock's 1928 song *The Big Rock Candy Mountain*. In those mountains:

There's a lake of stew, and of whiskey too
You can paddle all around 'em in a big canoe

Since Haywire Mac knew Joe Hill, and even recorded *The Preacher and the Slave*, it is possible that some of the inspiration for *The Big Rock Candy Mountain* came from Hill's *Preacher*.

The term 'pie in the sky' appeared first in *The Preacher and the Slave* by Joe Hill. Joe is duly credited with the invention in the 2009 edition of *Brewer's Dictionary of Phrase and Fable*, where 'pie in the sky' is defined as 'The good time or the good things promised that will never come; that which will never be realised'. The entry in *Brewer's* also includes the lyrics to the chorus of *The Preacher and the Slave*.

The second verse of the song replaces the 'long-haired preachers' with 'the starvation army'; evidently the Salvation Army. Although the Salvationists 'sing and they clap and they pray', they also promise 'pie in the sky'. The mention of the Army suggests that we are no longer listening to a preacher in a slave settlement: slavery was abolished in the U.S. in 1865, and the Salvationists did not start work in America until 1880. Hill's lyrics make it clear that the Christian hypocrites, including the Salvationists and the 'Holy Rollers and

Jumpers', are still active – they do not just belong way back in the days of slavery. They continue to tell people who:

> . . . fight hard for children and wife
> Try to get something good in this life

that they are bad men, and will surely go to hell.

The end of *The Preacher and the Slave* implies that 'workingmen of all countries' should ignore the Christian hypocrites, unite, fight for freedom, seize 'the world and its wealth' and, to feed themselves in this life, learn 'how to cook and to fry'.

Hill's insistence here that 'workingmen' should learn to cook is a reminder that he himself knew his way round a kitchen. He was notable for preparing meals in the Chinese style, though it is unclear where he could have picked up such a skill. We know that he spent time in San Francisco, which had an important Chinese community both before and after the 1906 earthquake, so perhaps it was there that Hill learned. He enjoyed cooking Chinese for friends who needed a meal, but he must have sought out Chinatowns in various North American cities to source ingredients to make his meals more authentic. For hobo guests, Joe's stir-frys must have been a welcome change from the 'mulligans' of the hobo jungles.

Like many of Hill's songs, *The Preacher and the Slave* seems to be directed primarily at a male audience. As we have seen, *There is Power in a Union* tells us that 'There is pow'r there is pow'r in a band of *workingmen*'. We have also seen how in *Where the Fraser River Flows* Hill addresses the railway construction workers on strike in Yale, British Columbia as 'boys'.

Joe Hill evidently understood how women had contributed to the IWW cause: how could he not? Women were essential to the success of two of the most celebrated IWW strikes: the Lawrence, Massachusetts strike of textile workers, and the 1913 strike of silk workers in Paterson, New Jersey. Hill's 1915 song *The Rebel Girl*, which for once is set to Hill's own, original tune, and was either completed or entirely written in prison in Salt Lake, sounds like Joe's attempt to rebalance his song-book with some recognition of the female contribution to the cause of labour:

Yes, her hands may be hardened from labour,
And her dress may not be very fine;
But a heart in her bosom is beating
That is true to her class and her kind.
And the grafters in terror are trembling
When her spite and defiance she'll hurl;
For the only and thoroughbred lady
Is the Rebel Girl.

In fact in one of his prison letters Hill told his friend Sam Murray that he hoped *The Rebel Girl* would 'help to line up the women workers in the OBU'.

The verse printed above evokes a poorly-dressed girl working in some grim industrial setting, but Hill was clear that *The Rebel Girl* was inspired by the aforementioned Elizabeth Gurley Flynn, a prominent early Wobbly who was one of the leading organisers of the strikes in Lawrence and Paterson.

Hill often wrote to her from prison, calling her 'Gurley', which was actually her mother's maiden surname.

Joe's correspondent was the child of radical Irish parents, born in Concord, New Hampshire in 1890, making her eleven years younger than Hill. At sixteen she was expelled from her school in New York for delivering a speech called 'What Socialism Will Do for Women'. At seventeen, she was already organising full-time for the IWW, although she was no Polyanna when it came to the American unions. She criticised them for being too male-dominated, and worked for feminist issues such as birth-control and votes for women.

In 1920 Elizabeth Gurley Flynn became a founding member of the American Civil Liberties Union (ACLU) which is still very much alive and kicking, and in 1961 she became national chairperson of the Communist Party of the United States. She died during a visit to Russia in 1964. Remembering how Hill had written *The Rebel Girl* for her forty years earlier, Elizabeth called her 1955 autobiography *I Speak My Own Piece: Autobiography of the "Rebel Girl"*.

In a recording of a speech by Gurley Flynn, she confirmed that the song was written for her, and added that 'if there is one thing that I am really proud of' it was 'her' Joe Hill song. She concluded that 'it may not be the best of words, or the best of music, but it came from the heart, and it was certainly so treasured'.

It is natural that the life and death of Joe Hill the songwriter should have inspired other people to write songs about him. *Joe Hill*, also called *I Dreamed I saw Joe Hill Last Night,* has words by Alfred Hayes (1925) and music by Earl Robinson (added in 1936). *When* the words and music came together is significant: the song appeared in the middle of the

Great Depression (1929-1939), when widespread unemployment brought dire poverty and social unrest, particularly in America. The song's fervent pro-union sentiments must have sounded particularly defiant during those desperate times.

The song imagines that something like the ghost of Joe Hill has visited the singer in a dream. Naturally the singer challenges the ghost, saying, 'But Joe, you're ten years dead' (which would have been the case when Hayes wrote the lyrics in 1925). Joe's ghost replies, 'I never died'. The singer goes on to tell Joe's ghost *how* he died: 'in Salt Lake City . . . they framed you on a murder charge . . . the copper bosses killed you', but still Joe insists 'I ain't dead'.

As we have seen, the direct involvement of the Utah 'copper bosses' in Joe Hill's death is hard to prove. It is, however, likely that at least some members of Hill's jury, the state governor, and other officials in the Mormon state were anti-union on principle, and tended to think of all unions as just as bad as each other. They also saw bodies such as the IWW and individuals such as Joe Hill as threats to good order and prosperity (or to their beloved system of oppression and exploitation, depending on your point of view).

In the song, Joe Hill's ghost expands on the idea that, despite his execution, he isn't dead. 'What they forgot to kill', he explains, 'went on to organise'. This means that 'where working men are out on strike' Joe Hill 'is at their side . . . from San Diego up to Maine, | In every mine and mill'.

While he says this, the Joe of Hayes's lyrics is 'smiling with his eyes'. This suggests that the lyricist had a particular photo of Hill at hand or in his mind when he wrote the words to the song. In the famous picture where the doomed Wobbly has a dark hat pushed far back on his head, Joe is certainly smiling with his eyes.

My own introduction to Joe Hill as a working-class hero came when I heard a recording of *I Dreamed I saw Joe Hill Last Night* by the American singer Paul Robeson (1898-1976). In fact Robeson was much more than just a singer, although his fine bass-baritone voice made him one of the best of his generation. He was an actor, playing the title role in Shakespeare's *Othello* in three different productions, and also an important left-wing political activist. His communist sympathies meant that he was frequently harassed by the US authorities, and often sought sanctuary in Britain. A single of Robeson singing *Joe Hill*, with *John Brown's Body* on the B-side, was released in the UK in 1956.

Another notable rendition of the Joe Hill song was given by Joan Baez at the famous Woodstock music festival in 1969. 'Woodstock', as it has become known, was one of those events that can happen unexpectedly, but which come to define a period, a movement or a generation, or mark an important cultural shift. The death of President John F. Kennedy was certainly such a moment, as was Martin Luther King's 'I have a dream' speech, given in Washington DC in 1963.

In our own century, the death of George Floyd in police custody in Minneapolis in 2020, and the storming of the US Capitol by Trump supporters in the following year, have become similarly defining moments. Such iconic events become more significant as time puts more years between us and them, and they are endlessly discussed and re-examined.

Woodstock was a festival that could have spiralled into violent chaos. The organisers had expected around fifty thousand spectators: in the event, over *four hundred thousand* turned up, many taking advantage of the fact that nobody could be kept out, so that possession of such a thing as a ticket became irrelevant.

While some elements of the media were keen to characterise Woodstock as an almighty mess, the gentle spirit of many of the attenders turned it into a triumph for peace and love. Whether the business of organising workplace unions was uppermost in the minds of any of the Woodstock festival-goers is unclear. On stage just before one o'clock in the morning of the second day, Joan Baez attempted to link the struggles of people like Joe Hill to the grievances of her own generation. At the time, her husband David Harris was in prison for refusing to be drafted into the US army to fight in Vietnam. Before she sang *Joe Hill*, which she called 'an organising song', Baez explained that in jail her husband had organised a hunger strike involving forty-two of his fellow-prisoners, none of whom had been locked up for dodging the draft, as he had.

Baez's 'take' on Joe Hill at Woodstock was slow and mournful – she made it very much a song about a dead man. Her high, arresting vibrato voice conferred a kind of classic nobility on what is on one level a simple folk song. Her facial expression throughout was suitably gloomy – she was, after all, not only singing about the loss of a working-class hero: she was also six months pregnant by a man who was deliberately starving himself in jail. She sang *Joe Hill* standing alone with just an acoustic guitar, surrounded by utter blackness, among the puddles on-stage that had been left by one of the showers and rain-storms that plagued the festival.

Joe Hill was one of fourteen songs Joan Baez performed at Woodstock, in a set that went on until two in the morning. The

1970 documentary film about the festival got Baez noticed, and her link to the legendary event has continued to do her career no end of good.

Another anti-Vietnam-war protest gesture seen and heard at Woodstock was Jimi Hendrix's instrumental version of *The Star-Spangled Banner* played on an electric guitar. Hendrix interspersed the patriotic tune with stunning sound-effects of bombs dropping and fighter-jets screeching, all done on the guitar, evoking a mental picture of the US flag spattered with blood, shrapnel and napalm.

The Myth

The myth of Joe Hill, as encapsulated in the song by Hayes and Robinson, has extraordinary power, and it is natural to ask, '*Why* is it so powerful?' Some of its power may derive from the similarities between Joe Hill's myth and the central myth of Western culture, the story of Jesus (I mean 'myth' here in the sense of 'powerful story' rather than 'falsehood' or 'lie': this is not the place to go into what actually happened to Jesus, whether he really existed, or anything like that).

A link between Jesus and Joe was made explicit in the mural by Mary Lathrop that was painted onto the wall of a homeless shelter called Joe Hill House in Salt Lake City. Founded by Lathrop and a Christian Wobbly called Ammon Hennacy in 1961, the House closed down in 1968. The mural only survives as a black and white photograph, but one can see that it resembles some paintings by the Mexican artist Frida Kahlo, and pictures in the Mexican *retablo* tradition that inspired the celebrated Frida.

Retablos, small devotional scenes often painted onto tin, usually show figures like the Virgin Mary floating down from heaven to intervene in the lives of ordinary people, working

101

much-needed miracles, for instance of healing. Lathrop may have drawn on the *retablo* tradition because Joe Hill House was a product of the Catholic Worker Movement. Her Joe Hill mural was like a *retablo* in that it showed the crucified Christ, complete with halo, hovering over a scene showing the execution of Hill. Christ is emerging from a circle of clouds, and his feet are surrounded by flames. These additions to the usual crucifixion iconography may have been inspired by the New Testament Book of Revelation, where we learn that the feet of Christ are 'like unto fine brass, as if they burned in a furnace' (Revelation 1:15, King James Version) and that 'he cometh with the clouds' (1:17).

The fact that in the mural both Jesus and Joe were shown attached to structures on which they would die (a cross and a chair respectively) suggests that the artist may have been thinking of the similarities between them, but her picture might also have been designed to suggest that the crucified Jesus was descending into the execution scene because of his boundless compassion, and his anger about what was happening.

Whether Mary Lathrop was trying to indicate parallels between Christ and the Wobbly troubadour is unclear, but such parallels certainly exist. Both Joe and Jesus were unjustly executed by the state, but both defied death – Jesus rising from the dead and ascending bodily into heaven, and Joe going on to inspire Americans 'from San Diego up to Maine' as they try to 'strike and organise'. The implication of Hayes's words in the Joe Hill song is that workers who gather together to try to found a union will be visited by that part of Joe Hill that could not be killed by guns. This is remarkably reminiscent of

Jesus's assertion that 'where two or three are gathered together in my name, there am I in the midst of them' (Matthew 18:20).

Although the body of Jesus is supposed to have ascended into Heaven, the ceremony of the Eucharist re-enacts the symbolic consumption of his body and blood: one thinks of Billy Bragg consuming a pinch of Joe's ashes, not with communion wine but with union beer.

Like Joe Hill, Jesus, who could be astoundingly eloquent, was taciturn when it came to defending himself against the accusers who ultimately killed him. The evidence would suggest that both accepted their respective executions as in some way inevitable. In this, both resembled the ancient Greek philosopher Socrates, who calmly responded to being found guilty of impiety by agreeing to take poison.

Both Joe and Jesus suffered harsh treatment and imprisonment before they were murdered, and both made many enemies, even among people who had never met them. Many right-wingers and enthusiasts for capitalism hated people like Hill on principle, and one suspects that many at the top of both the Roman and Jewish hierarchies in first-century Palestine would have felt uneasy about the continued existence of an unconventional prophet who seemed to be gathering new followers every day.

Despite their enemies, both Joe and Jesus had loyal followers who wrote good things about them after they died. Both continued to be significant, in the IWW and among the early Christians, respectively. All over the world, people sing about Jesus, and passages in the Gospels are sung, as are Joe Hill's songs.

There are other striking similarities between the two men, although some Christians, and left-wingers with an aversion to

Christianity, might find the naming of these similarities offensive. Both came from distant places to teach benighted people about a new way to live; Joe from Sweden, and Jesus from Nazareth, an obscure village over sixty miles from Jerusalem, where the crucial action of the Jesus story occurred. Neither had made much of an impression at home: as Jesus said, a prophet is never honoured in his own country (John 4:44).

Both had extraordinary gifts, Joe as a songwriter and Jesus as a teacher and miracle-worker. Both also went by several names: Joe was also Joseph and Joel, Hillstrom and Hägglund; and Jesus is also known as Christ, Emmanuel, Yeshua, the Saviour, Pantera and the Nazarene, among other names. The fact that Joel Hägglund probably changed his name before he became an influential figure is reminiscent of the Old Testament patriarch Abraham, who had to leave his home in Mesopotamia and change his name from Abram.

Both Joe and Jesus were proficient in more than one language; Joe in Swedish and English, and Jesus (probably) in Hebrew, Aramaic, Greek and perhaps Latin. Both were killed in their thirties, and neither is known to have been married or fathered children. Both also travelled across huge distances during the most active parts of their lives. Even Joe Hill's habit of cooking for his friends is reminiscent of the episode where Jesus cooks fish for his disciples (John 21:9).

Those who resent any attempt to compare an early twentieth-century union agitator to the Christian messiah might feel slightly more comfortable with the idea that both Jesus and Joe Hill shared characteristics with a heroic archetype that is found in contexts beyond politics and Christianity, some of which pre-date Christianity by several centuries. We have already heard about Socrates. Like Jesus, the Buddha, who may have been a contemporary of Socrates, made enemies but found disciples, inspired his listeners and achieved a kind of immortality. Like Hill, Jesus and Abraham, the Buddha had to leave his own country before he began to make an impact, and he is also known by several names, including Gautama and Siddhartha.

The figure of Orpheus in ancient Greek mythology is even older than Socrates and the Buddha. Like Joe Hill, Orpheus was a gifted musician and composer – he could charm animals, trees and even rocks with his music. According to some versions of the Orpheus myth, he was killed when he was torn to pieces by Thracian women, which is reminiscent of the division of Joe Hill's ashes after his death. Other heroes who were torn to pieces were the Egyptian god Osiris, the Finnish hero Lemminkäinen and the Northumbrian king and saint Oswald, whose body was split up by his enemies after his death in battle.

Like Joe Hill's ashes, Oswald's body-parts were disposed of in different places. In the Joe Hill song, the dead activist appears to the singer in a dream: something similar happened to St Oswald on the eve of the Battle of Heavenfield early in the seventh century. On this occasion, the Northumbrian king was greatly encouraged by a dream-visit from the long-dead Irish saint, Columba.

When it comes to saints, it might be said that Joe Hill's letters from prison resemble those sent by the apostle Paul during his own incarceration. The way Joe appears in a dream to the singer of the Joe Hill song also resembles the challenging vision of Jesus that came to Paul (then called Saul) on the road to Damascus. The visionary Jesus who appears to

Saul at this time assures the future saint that he is still alive in some way, and can continue to influence events in the world of the living (see Acts chapter 9).

Of course the (sometimes illiterate) workers struggling to build unions in the thirties, who were inspired by Hayes and Robinson's song about Joe Hill, would not necessarily have known about Orpheus, Osiris, Oswald, the Buddha or Socrates; but many of them would have known about Jesus, and if their journey towards socialism was taking them away from Christianity, they may have been looking to use figures like Joe Hill as a kind of substitute for Jesus, and the Christian saints and martyrs who tried to follow his example.

It might be said that those who gained control of the Soviet Union attempted to convert Vladimir Lenin into a kind of communist messiah. Lenin also came from a remote place (his exile in Western Europe) to teach the Russians a new way to live. He also changed his name (from Vladimir Ulyanov) as did Stalin and Trotsky; he also had enemies (one of whom shot and nearly killed him in 1918) and he lived on in Soviet propaganda, his own writings, statues and paintings. For many years, his embalmed body was even displayed in a special shrine outside the Kremlin in Moscow, like the body or body-parts of a Christian saint displayed as relics in a church or cathedral.

For many people the modern substitute for the myths and legends of old are films and written fiction, particularly in the science fiction and fantasy genres. These often draw self-consciously on ancient tales, even from the Bible, and they appeal to millions who know little or nothing about Jesus, Buddha or the ancient Greeks. This suggests that myths that follow the Jesus-Buddha-Orpheus-Osiris-Joe Hill model appeal to something deep in the human psyche, something pre-literate and perhaps even deeper than culture itself.

Luke Skywalker, the hero of the early Star Wars films, has to leave his home planet to make an impact on his far-away galaxy, and is clearly adept at languages, even the languages spoken by the films' 'droids' or robots. He has special powers, which are brought out by his mentor, the wizard-like Obi-Wan Kenobi. In one scene, Luke seems to come back from the dead, after being trapped under some garbage-filled water for rather longer than most people could hold their breaths. He even bounces back unscathed from the loss of his hand, which is restored not by magic or a miracle, but by the advanced technology of the Star Wars universe.

In Frank Herbert's 1965 science-fiction novel *Dune*, the young hero Paul Atreides only begins to gain significance and hero-status when he leaves his home planet of Caladan. He endures tragic losses and much hardship, but despite many threats against his life he acquires allies on the desert-planet of Arrakis, where the indigenous Fremen begin to regard him as a kind of messiah. Like Joe Hill, Jesus and Buddha, Paul acquires new names: Muad'Dib, the Lisan al-Gaib, the Mahdi and the Kwisatz Haderach. He also has super-human powers.

Although it seems that many people respond to, and perhaps need, heroes with mythical and legendary attributes, there are real historical people lurking somewhere inside some of the larger-than-life figures of myth and legend. Does the mythology obscure the reality? Do mythical elements attach themselves to the world's perception of important figures, and for no rational reason?

In Robert Silverberg's 1970 science-fiction novel *Tower of Glass* Simeon Krug, an insanely rich man who has created a race of androids to serve the people of the world, discovers that the androids have started to worship him as a kind of saviour, who will eventually grant them equal status with human beings. He goes to great lengths to convince the androids that he has no intention of saving or redeeming them from anything: the result is utter chaos and mayhem.

Perhaps, in the case of characters like Joe Hill, who may himself have been responsible for creating some of the mythology that is now attached to him, the hero is created by people who badly need a hero to inspire them. The mythical Joe Hill was constructed out of the raw material that was the short, tragic life of the IWW agitator.

But should people need heroes? The Victorian writer Thomas Carlyle published his influential *On Heroes, Hero-Worship and the Heroic in History* in 1841. The book offers a massive thumbs-up for hero-worship and affirms people's need for it; but some of the (all-male) heroes Carlyle offers for adoration are hard to warm to. Notoriously, the French philosopher Jean-Jacques Rousseau gave his own children away to a foundling hospital, and some would count Oliver Cromwell and Napoleon Bonaparte as mass-murderers, not heroes.

The hero issue is discussed in the left-wing German playwright Bertolt Brecht's play *Galileo* (1938). When someone comments that a land must indeed be unhappy if it has no heroes, Galileo responds by saying that a land that *needs* heroes must be the most unhappy. But then again, a working class hero is something to be.

Bibliography

Adler, William: *The Man Who Never Died,* Bloomsbury, 2012

Andersson, Ingvar: *A History of Sweden*, Praeger, 1956

Brecht, Bertolt: *Galileo*, Bloomsbury Methuen, 2013

Carlyle, Thomas: *On Heroes, Hero-Worship and the Heroic in History,* Yale, 2013

Cole, Peter: *Ben Fletcher: The Life and Times of a Black Wobbly*, PM Press, 2020

Devitt, Steve: *The Pen That Set Mexico on Fire*, Henselstone Verlag LLC, 2017

Giovanitti, Arturo: *Arrows in the Gale*, Quale, 2004

Green, Archie (ed.): *The Big Red Songbook*, PM Press, 2016

Gurley Flynn, Elizabeth: *I Speak My Own Piece: Autobiography of the "Rebel Girl",* International, 1973

Haywood, William D.: *Bill Haywood's Book: The Autobiography of William D. Haywood*, Papamoa, 2018

Herbert, Frank: *Dune*, Hodder, 2021

Ibsen, Henrik: *A Doll's House*, Methuen, 2020

Knight, Alan: *The Mexican Revolution: A Very Short Introduction*, Oxford, 2016

Kornbluh, Joyce L (ed.): *Rebel Voices: An IWW Anthology*, Charles Kerr, 1985

Kropotkin, Peter: *The Conquest of Bread*, Read & Co., 2020

Little Botkin, Jane: *Frank Little and the IWW*, University of Oklahoma Press, 2017

London, Jack: *Five Great Short Stories*, Dover, 2000

Marx, Karl: *Capital*, Fingerprint, 2016

Marx, Karl and Engels, Frederick (ed. Feuer, Lewis S (ed.): *Basic Writings on Politics and Philosophy*, Fontana, 1969

Rosemont, Franklin: *Joe Hill: The IWW & the Making of a Revolutionary Workingclass Counterculture,* PM Press, 2015

Safstrom, Mark: *The Religious Origins of Democratic Pluralism,* Pickwick, 2016

Safstrom, Mark (ed.) *The Swedish Pietists: A Reader*, Pickwick, 2015

Silverberg, Robert: *Tower of Glass*, Gateway, 2011

Smith, Gibbs: *Joe Hill*, Gibbs Smith, 1969

Strindberg, August: *Miss Julie and Other Plays*, Oxford, 1998

Strindberg, August: *The Red Room*, Lector, 2019

Turner, Ethel Duffy: *Revolution in Baja California: Ricardo Flores Magón's High Noon,* Blaine/Ethridge, 1981

Turner, John Kenneth: *Barbarous Mexico*, Alpha, 2020

Waldenström, Paul Petter: *Squire Adamsson*, Pietisten, 2014

For more from the Langley Press, please visit our new website at www.langleypress.co.uk

Printed in Great Britain
by Amazon

19263302R00068